THE PRAYER INSPIRED LIFE

THE PRAYER INSPIRED LIFE

Michael L. McCann, Ed. D., N.D.

Dr. Michael L. McCann
P.O. Box 1386
Bay City, MI 48706

24 hour Internet TV channel:
www.prayerinspired.tv

Join Dr. McCann and other guests for prayer and teaching on prayer. Your life will never be the same as you learn to pray with authority, knowledge and power. Watch www.prayerinspired.tv anytime of day or night online 24 hours a day.

Website:
www.doctormccann.com

Copyright © 2006 by Michael L. McCann, Ed. D., N.D.

ISBN 1-56229-050-9

Pneuma Life Publishing
P. O. Box 10612
Lanham, MD 20721
1-800-727-3218
www.pneumalife.com

Printed in the United States of America. All rights reserved under International Copyright Law. Contents and/or cover may not be reproduced in whole or in part in any form without the express written consent of the publisher.

Dedication

This book is dedicated to my faithful prayer partner, Rita, my wife. Through the years together, we have prayed over countless things and have seen the hand of God move in impossible situations. Together we have witnessed numerous miracles of healing and many glorious conversions to our Lord Jesus Christ. Without her gracious help this book, **The Prayer Inspired Life,** would not be possible.

Table of Contents

Preface
Introduction

Chapter		
1	God	11
2	God the Creator	15
3	Creation	21
4	Humankind Made in His Image and Likeness	25
5	Relationship	29
6	God's Love for You	33
7	God is a Good God	37
8	God is Able	41
9	Trusting God	45
10	Faith in God's Ability	49
11	The Infallible Word	53
12	Seeking God	57
13	Abiding in Him	63

14	The Reverence of God	69
15	Heart, Mind and Soul	73
16	How to Love God	77
17	What is Prayer?	83
18	Sovereign Intervention	89
19	Delayed Prayer	93
20	Prayer of Agreement	99
21	Praying Continuously	103
22	Common Sense and Prayer	107
23	Intercessory Prayer	111
24	Prayer and Fasting	115
25	Claiming Your Promises	121
26	Watch Your Mouth	125
27	Battle of the Mind	129
28	The Prayer of Commitment	133
29	Avoiding Thomas	139
30	Hearing the Voice of the Holy Spirit	143
31	Open Heaven	149

Bibliography

Footnotes

Preface

Our nation cries out for a revival of the Holy Spirit. Yet, very few churches are experiencing an out-pouring of the Spirit here in the United States. Unfortunately there is a creeping coldness in many churches that were at one time very much on fire for the Lord. It is obvious man has made his plans for church growth without the consultation of the Holy Spirit.

Without the Holy Spirit's leading in today's churches, only some people are being attracted to the Church while multitudes should be clamoring at the doors to get in. Prayer and its power have been omitted from the Church. We have well-educated and trained clergy who know all about psychology, counseling and theology, but they lack the power of the Spirit.

The purpose of this prayer manual is to once again stress the need of prayer in the Church. The average church member will find new zeal in their spiritual lives as they put into practice the prayer aspects found in this manual. The Prayer Inspired Life has been written for those who desire to go on with God into greater realms of glory. It will change the average Christian into a mature Christian. He or she will find greater peace, power, and purpose as a result of putting into practice a Prayer Inspired Life.

This prayer manual teaches truths that have worked for the last two thousand years. May we all come to that place where we adopt the principles of the Prayer Inspired Life. I believe once we get back to prayer in our Churches, they will be filled to capacity. The harvest is waiting to come in, but only prayer can make it happen.

Introduction

Prayer is perhaps the greatest unused source of power in our entire universe. It has been available for use by Christians for over two thousand years and yet it still remains a great mystery to many of us. For those who tap into its energy, it has shown to be an amazing tool to change the unchangeable. There are dimensions to prayer that many have never contemplated. Knowing the right way to pray can cover all of the needs of humanity. Nevertheless, prayer remains an unused source of energy to countless multitudes.

It is the intent of this book to study the major areas of prayer and to connect with the supernatural in a most miraculous way. Our Lord Jesus Christ desires to speak to us. He is much closer than what many of us have known and realize. We will come to know Him in a deep new way as we learn the art of prayer. We can sit at His feet on a daily basis as we pray earnestly to Him. He will answer and even begin to speak to us in our souls.

This book is intended to be a therapeutic understanding of the supernatural involving the many different ways of praying. Prayer is much more than asking as we oftentimes do when we seek our Lord. There is a dimension of prayer that very few ever reach. Let us come together and see how far we can go into the supernatural world of prayer. There will be various spiritual exercises in prayer at the end of each chapter to aid and guide you on your way to becoming a most successful prayer warrior.

God

<u>My verse for today is</u>:
"**God is a Spirit: and they that worship him must worship him in spirit and in truth**" *(John 4:24)*.

The concept of God for many persons in the 21st Century is no longer a necessary or consistent part of their every day lives. Some live as though God does not exist, while many barely admit He is here. Unfortunately we have come to a place where we think God is not really needed today. For example, nowadays we have all kinds of new inventions that totally take over our time and energy. These gadgets have made the need for God a vague, abstract idea.

Yet, the God of Christians is omniscient, holy and very loving. Countless people believe God wants to speak to His children, but they do not take the opportunity to hear from Him or speak to Him. Christians believe God knows all about humanity's needs and sufferings and yet He is a holy God who cannot and will not excuse sin. In spite of our fallen nature, He desires to take humanity into fellowship with Him. He is a most kind and loving God who will put into operation a plan for each individual to find Him and salvation.

Christians believe God is omnipotent (all powerful) and will reveal Himself to those who truly seek Him. He has set into writing a profound revelation of His being. Christians call His writings "The Holy Bible." The Bible is considered inspired by the faithful and gives direction for those who seek a purpose and plan for their lives.

Despite God's love for all, He seems to remain hidden to a greater part of humanity. In Seminary, we studied Blaise Pascal who spoke of God as being hidden (Deus Absconditus). At the same time, Pascal believed and taught that God who has been hidden, does reveal Himself to those who seek Him. Pascal asserts that God can be known, even though at times He appears to be hidden.

It is neither possible nor practical to give an adequate definition of God. It is only in the Holy Scriptures that we are able to discern or ascertain Who God is. In the old Westminster Shorter Catechism, God is taught as being "A Spirit, infinite, eternal, and unchangeable, in His being, wisdom, power and holiness, justice, goodness, and truth." Yet each of us sees God differently in light of our understanding, background, education, and intellectual capabilities.

As one draws near to God, he sees his life remarkably different in the Bible from what he thought he would find. A man's life in the Word of God is almost like a romance, since he is told over and over again how much he is "accepted in the beloved." Ephesians 1:6 reads: ***"To the praise of the glory of his grace, wherein he hath made us accepted in the beloved."*** It does not matter who you are or how much money you may have, God is an eternal absolute who wants to communicate with you. Not only that, but He wants you to talk to Him.

For multitudes of people, it may seem that God hides Himself from them. In a certain sense, this is true. Isaiah 45:15 says, *"Truly you are a God who hides himself."* We must learn to approach Him by faith, since our God sets a premium on His children who live by faith. As we begin to exercise our faith in Him, our numerous doubts will begin to disappear. Things that once held us back from coming to Him, all at once begin to disappear.

As we begin to share in the life of Jesus Christ, His Spirit begins to take our lives over. The scales are removed from our eyes, and we come out of the shadow lands into an active faith that is more real and alive than anything else in this life.

God wants to show us His love and graciousness. Isaiah 30:18 says, *"He rises to show you compassion."* This is so vividly demonstrated in Genesis 21:15-17, where we see Hagar and her son in absolute desperation dying in the desert, and the angel of the Lord ministers both water and life to them. *"And God heard the voice of the lad; and the angel of God called to Hagar out of heaven, and said unto her, What aileth thee, Hagar? fear not; for God hath heard the voice of the lad where he is."*

God wants to hear from you! There is a road to take that will bring peace, power and purpose in this life. We can come to the knowledge of God as we learn to talk to Him on this road of enlightenment. The great theologian, J. I. Packer once said, "Anyone who is actually following a recognized road will not be too worried if he hears non-travelers telling each other that no such road exists."[1][1]

Things to consider:

My road to spiritual enlightenment begins the day I choose to take this new road. Think about God each and every day. Start each morning with a conversation with Him. This is one of the many things you should ask of God.

God

<u>Pray something like this:</u>

God help me to come into that place where I can truly know that You exist by faith. Please help me to talk to You. Bless this new day with Your wonderful presence always with me and around me.

God the Creator

<u>My verse for today is</u>:
"In whom also we have obtained an inheritance, being predestinated according to the purpose of him who worketh all things after the counsel of his own will" *(Ephesians 1:11)*.

Where did it all begin? The Christian believes that God is the author of all Creation. Genesis 1:1 says, ***"In the beginning God created the heaven and the earth."*** It would appear that all of history might be found in this verse.

Do we know the exact date of the creation of heaven and earth? Through the centuries, Christians and non-Christians alike have attempted to find the date of Creation but to no avail. Trying to date the first day of Creation is virtually impossible. We must believe by faith that God created everything, and that all of it is good.

In Seminary, we studied a man by the name of Rt. Rev. James Usher (1581-1656). He was an Irish bishop whose theory says Creation began in the early morning of the twenty-third of October 4004 B.C. He used the Julian calendar of 710 to arrive at his theory, which was taught in European seminaries for numerous centuries. It became so popular that many of the old editions of the King James Bible show his Creation theory in the margins of its text. Consequently, it began to have some kind of divine "significance."

"In the beginning God created the heaven and the earth." It is from this Scripture that we ascertain the next six days of Creation (Genesis 1:3-31). As we study the Bible, we see an order to all that is around us. It did not happen by mere chance. There was a divine plan and purpose. The first part of Creation formed the structure of Creation itself. The second part of Creation was filling Creation with every kind of life. God did this for us, so we might come to know Him as the being He really is.

As we study the Creation narrative, we find that on the first day God created light. **"And God called the light Day, and the darkness he called Night. And the evening and the morning were the first day"** (Genesis 1:5). All in one day, God did this most wonderful act so mankind could tell the time of day.

Now on the second day, God took a world full of water and gave it definition. On the very first day all that could be seen was water in the light, but on the second day there could be seen a glorious sky, differentiated from the waters.

On the third day, we read, **"And God said, Let the waters under the heaven be gathered together unto one place, and let the dry land appear: and it was so."** Dry ground appeared as the seas and oceans were put into their special place. God called the day places "land" and the gathered waters "seas." It is on this particular day that **"God saw that it was good"** (Genesis 1:10).

During the latter half of the third day, God made the land productive with fruit-growing trees and countless seed-bearing plants. Can you imagine how many seed-bearing plants were created? All kinds of abundant vegetation came into existence at this particular moment in time. Again God said what He created was "good."

Now on the fourth day, His most infinite intelligence is at work again in a most dynamic way. Here He begins the second phase of His Creation. Taking into consideration the first day, God creates the two "great lights." Here we see that the greater light is given to govern the day, and the lesser of the two lights to govern the night (Genesis 1:16). The greater lights were placed in the sky to divide the signs of the seasons as well as to function to differentiate the day from the night. During this day, the stars were also created for the purpose of giving men great joy. Again God *"saw that it was good"* (Genesis 1:18).

On the fifth day God, our Creator, filled the seas and the air with every kind of living creature one could possibly imagine. The *"great whales, and every living creature that moveth, which the waters brought forth abundantly, after their kind, and every winged fowl after his kind: and God saw that it was good"* (Genesis 1:21). The great sea creatures and "every winged bird" were created, blessed, and ordered to increase in their number. Everything He has created is good in His own eyes, and it is with this attitude that we must approach Him. He is a good God who enjoys His Creation, and we are a special part of His Creation. God so longs for us to communicate with Him. He takes great pleasure in knowing that He has made a way through Jesus Christ, that we might once again talk to Him and He to us.

On the sixth day, God created His most important Creation. It is on this day that man came into being. He made the human race and took abundant joy in creating mankind. **"Let us make man in our image, after our likeness"** (Genesis 1:26). Man is the pinnacle of all of God's Creation. God gave man authority to rule over the living creatures in the sky, the sea and even on land. And God told Adam and Eve to increase in their numbers, too. Man made in the image and likeness of God was given total dominion to rule over God's Creation. What a profound privilege He gave all of mankind.

There is a particular phrase in the Creation narrative that we must look at a little closer, which is: ***"Let us make man in our image...."*** It is here that we get our first impression of the Godhead or the Trinity of God. Again, He is also referring to the countless number of angels in heaven who are watching Him and what He is doing with His spoken word.

On the sixth day of Creation, God gave humankind and the animal kingdom something from which to receive nourishment. He gave man every ***"seed-bearing plant...and every tree that has fruit with seed in it"*** to eat (Genesis 1:29). To the animal kingdom, He gave the rest of the vegetation - every green plant. It is recorded in Scripture that God made vegetation during the latter part of the second day. We see on the sixth day, God gave Adam and every living creature the necessary foods for survival.

At the end of the sixth day, God took a careful look at what He created. He saw that ***"It was very good"*** (Genesis 1:31). Now begins chapter 2 and God's ultimate thought on His Creation: ***"Thus the heavens and the earth were finished, and all the host of them"*** (Gen. 2:1). Man begins his life living in the splendor of the Garden of Eden. In Hebrew, the word, "Eden" means "a place of delight." Many Bible scholars believe the Garden of Eden was located at the eastern end of the fertile Mesopotamian Crescent, near where the Tigris and Euphrates Rivers meet.

Adam and Eve were the first of all human beings. The Bible speaks of a deep sleep that came upon Adam, and during his sleep, God took one of Adam's ribs and then closed the wound. Woman was then created from Adam's very own rib. When the Septuagint Translators transcribed the Bible into Greek, the Hebrew word, "tsela" in Genesis 2, became "pleura." However, this is not very accurate. It is only in the plural form that "pleura" refers to a set of ribs.[1] [2] The most common translation is "side" and in Adam's case, it is the "side of man." It is even possible that the term refers to the "wife" as the Hebrew "tsela," and it often means a bosom friend or a person who is at one's side.

The Christian faith affirms that all of creation came through the sovereign will of God. At the same time, God still transcends all that He has created. It is this same God who wants to speak to us through prayer. Why are we so frightened to approach Him? Is it because He is so mighty and powerful beyond our wildest imagination?

In Seminary, I read some of the books of J. I. Parker who wrote:

> "We are cruel to our self if we try to live in this world without knowing about the God whose world it is and who runs it. The world becomes a strange mad, painful place and life in it a disappointing and unpleasant business for those who do not know about God. Disregard the study of God and you sentence yourself to stumble and blunder through life blindfolded, as it were, with no sense of direction and no understanding of what surrounds you."[2][3]

Things to consider:

I was not born by chance. I am alive by divine appointment. I am a child of destiny. I am a part of God's Creation having purpose and meaning for my life. Humbly praying to God will actually reveal my divine destiny.

Pray something like this:

Dear Father God, I really don't know You and I need understanding in how to talk to You. Please help me understand! In His name I pray. Amen.

Creation

<u>My verse for today is</u>:
"To the praise of the glory of his grace, wherein he hath made us accepted in the beloved" (*Ephesians* 1:6).

In the book of Genesis, we read about the cosmic creativity of God's Spirit in the creation of the universe and humankind. There is a broad spectrum of activity of God's Spirit in the Book of Genesis. He is in the act of all creation. We see His work from Creation, to judging, to restraining people from sin, to infilling leaders with wisdom and discernment. Later on in the Bible, we see God's providential care of His chosen people.

The initial mention of the Spirit of God in the Bible is in the second verse of chapter 1. Verse 1 serves as an opening statement about God's creation of the vast universe. Verse 2 describes the chaotic condition of the earth as "tohu" and "bohu," shapeless and without any kind of inhabitants. Then God speaks a series of authoritative commands (Genesis 1:3-31). At this early stage, **"the Spirit of God (Ruah Elohim) moves over the surface of the wa-**

ters." The Spirit of God is referred to "as a mighty wind" in this earliest account of Creation. Therefore, the Holy Spirit acts to bring forth order by preparing "the primeval formlessness" to hear the creative Word of God. The Spirit hovers over the waters waiting for further instructions.

In Genesis 1:2, we see God as the divine energizer preparing to create order and give design to the shapeless substance. He is preparing to create a universe to operate and display His glory. It is the transformation of a nonfunctioning universe into a functional universe filled with His glory that is about to transpire.

In the New Testament, it is interesting to note that the concept of God's hovering presence occurs in the angel's birth announcement to Mary: **"The Holy Spirit will overshadow (episkiasei) thee"** (Luke 1:35). The conception of Jesus Christ is the very first creative act of the new Creation.[1] [4] The same Greek word (episkzo) is used earlier in the Bible to describe God's glory cloud that once covered the tabernacle (Exodus 40:35 in the Septuagint). The Septuagint is the ancient Greek translation of the Old Testament.

Again in the New Testament we see a similar use of the same word with the cloud that overshadowed the Mount of Transfiguration (Matt. 17:5; Mark 9:7; Luke 9:34). By this glorious figure of the hovering and overshadowing presence of God's Spirit at the original Creation, the creation of Israel as a covenant nation and the new creation show how Jesus Christ links everything together. All things find themselves not only linked together but also fulfilled in Jesus Christ.

It is in Psalm 33:6, where we begin to see the profound implication of the Son of God at work in Creation. The Psalmist speaks of Him as the "the Word." It should be noted that this is the same expression that John uses in John 1:1-3 where the context again concerns the creation of God's universe. **"By the word of the Lord were the heavens made; and all the host of them by the breath of** *his mouth"* (Psalm 33:6). This infers "that all the heavenly bodies were made by a combined effort of the Son of God and the Spirit."[2] [5]

Genesis 1:26-27 finishes the Creation story with the ultimate creation of humankind (Hebrew Adam), both male and female. This is the last of God's greatest acts of creation. However, Genesis 2:4b-25 explains in detail, the creation of the first human couple by the "Lord God" (Yahweh Elohim).[3] [6] This is God's special name of Yahweh, which was first introduced to Moses in his dramatic encounter (Exodus 3:1-15; 6:2-8). Moses gives holy assurance to the Israelites that the same God who brought them out of Egypt is truly the Creator of the human race.

According to John Rhea in his book entitled The Holy Spirit in the Bible, Genesis 2:7 may be paraphrased, "And Yahweh God as a potter molded the (first) human (Adam) of clay dust from the ground (adamah), and He breathed strongly into his nostrils the breath of life (nismat, hayyim), and the first human (Adam) became a living being (nepes hayyim)."[4] [7]

There are several very important things to learn from the truths presented in Genesis 1:16-27 and 2:7. Man is a most special creation of the Almighty. While animals, birds and creeping things are called "living things" (1:20, 21, 24), only man is said to have been created in the image and likeness of God. This places the whole of humanity on a very special level, according to the Creation narrative. Humankind did not evolve gradually into its present state. Humankind, according to the Creation narrative, was created in one deliberate act, and only God could perform this stupendous act.

Not only did God create humankind to have bodies, He also gave us an eternal spirit and soul. It is very important to acknowledge and fully comprehend this wonderful truth: We are human spirits living in a fleshly body. Each of us has a body, which acts as a cover up to our eternal spirits. The Holy Spirit attempts to communicate to us through our spirits. This truth should help us in our prayer lives and our knowledge of who we are in Christ.

As we come to God in prayer, we realize we are "someone." We are not a mistake but a definite act of God's perfect will. Everyone who is living has been created with a positive intention for that life.

Things to consider:

I was created in the image and likeness of God. As I learn the skill and art of prayer, I will come to know the voice of the Holy Spirit. I am most precious to our Heavenly Father.

Pray something like this as you focus on God's love for you:

Heavenly Father, I want to know You and serve You with all of my heart. Holy Spirit, please lead me to the very heart of my Heavenly Father.

Humankind Made in His Image and Likeness

<u>My verse for today is</u>:
"For God so loved the world, that he gave his only begotten Son, that whosoever believeth in him should not perish, but have everlasting life" *(John 3:16)*.

In our study of prayer, I mentioned that man is made in the image and likeness of God. Man, having a spirit, soul and body, resembles God especially in His Spirit. Man has an eternal spirit that will live for all time. This is most noteworthy, since we determine our response to eternal life on this side of heaven.

Man is a created being made in the "image and likeness of God." God said, **"Let us make man in our image, after our likeness...."** (Genesis 1:26-27). There are two words, which we need to consider in our discussion of man. The words "create" and "make" are very significant. The word "make" means to fashion or form as a potter forms a vessel of clay. In Zechariah 12:1, we get a much better understanding of God's creation of man. It reads: **"The burden of the Word of the Lord for Israel, saith the Lord, which stretcheth forth the heavens, and layeth the foundation of the** *earth, and formeth the spirit of man within him."* Man is a created being. He owes his existence to God, Who not only gave him a body, but a spirit and soul as well.

Since man owes his existence to a Creator, this makes him a dependent creature. He is not self-existent and surely is not independent. Man is totally dependent upon God whether he knows this or not. Acts 17:28-31 tells us that in God *"we live, and move, and have our being."* Man is a most unique being having reason, intelligence, imagination, and the ability to express his thoughts in purposeful language. Man is a moral being since God gave him free will and the ability to choose. It is this, which makes man a moral and responsible creature. God created the angelic world with free will, and He created man in like manner. The human race was not created like a robot, machine, or will-less creature. God wanted a creature who would respond to Him with willingness and total freedom. Because sin entered the world through Adam and Eve's disobedience, man's will has been weakened. However, this does not deny that man still has a free will. Though man's free will has been corrupted and has an evil heart, he still is able to respond to God if he desires.

So man is capable of choices. Therefore man is capable of love. Here we come to the purpose and reason for our creation. God is love, and love must have an intended object. At the same time, love requires reciprocation. Man is capable of loving God with his entire being if he wishes to do so. The created universe, with its profound glory, cannot respond to God or His love. Only humankind is capable of such tenderness and adoration. If God is love and has created man in His own image, it is apparent that He wants man to reciprocate it. Man was created by the love of God and has a will to love God back for His kindness and gentleness. If man cannot love God, man's heart remains empty, deplete and void.

Man is considered by most theologians to be a trinity, having a spirit, soul and body. It is in the spirit that man has a God-consciousness; this makes man capable of knowing God. When God formed man, He gave man a spirit within him (Zechariah 12:1). Consequently, God is the God of all spirits (Numbers 16:22; 27:16; Hebrews 12:9). It is the spirit of man that is able to worship God who is a Spirit (John 4:24). Within the spirit of man are contained certain important faculties such as intuition, conscience and communion. When man fell into sin, he lost his ability to make contact with God. When man seeks God through Jesus Christ, it is then that he sees the need for prayer.

The soul is considered to be the self-conscious part of man. By that, it is meant that man is capable of knowing himself. Moses, in the account of Creation tells how God created man's body from the dust of the earth and then breathed into him "the breath of life" or more accurately breathed in the "breath of lives" (Genesis 2:7). The soul is the central part of man's being, which connects the spirit and the body together in trinity, similar to God's Trinity. The soul has the ability to influence the spirit and the body, because of its ability to connect with  both spirit and body. Man has been created with free will to do whatever he desires. At the same time, man was created to take delight and pleasure in knowing God. It is a choice that each one of us will have to make one day. To serve God or not to serve God, that is the question!

We have been created to have fellowship with our Heavenly Father. He wants all of us to have fellowship with Him. He delights when we take the time to worship Him. We are living creatures who have been created to live for all time. While we are still in the body, we need to take the opportunity to speak with our Creator. He wants to hear from each of us. Isn't it time to start speaking to your loving Creator? He's ready, willing and patiently waiting...

<u>Things to consider:</u>

I was created with purpose and intention in the mind of God. He absolutely loves His Creation. He sees all humankind as an object of adoration. He desires to have fellowship with each one of us. That fellowship begins when we start talking to Him.

Pray something like this:

Dear Heavenly Father, please help me to talk to You! At times I find it hard to believe that You love me so very much. Help me to come to that place where I really know You. In His name I pray. Amen.

Relationship

<u>My verse for today is</u>:
"But as many as received him, to them gave he power to become the sons of God, even to them that believe on his name" *(John 1:12)*.

It is through the person of Jesus Christ that we come to have a personal relationship with our Heavenly Father. In the Old Testament, God is known as Jehovah, and on other occasions the patriarchs would use glorious names such as God Almighty, and Lord of Heaven and Earth. There was no clear distinction of God's fatherhood until Jesus Christ appeared on the scene. It is in the New Testament that we come to know Him as a merciful and benevolent Being. Jesus Christ introduces us to His Heavenly Father. Here we come to see Him in a brand new light and dimension.

In Matthew 6:9, Jesus Christ begins the Lord's Prayer with **"Our Father which art in heaven, Hallowed be thy name."** The Lord's Prayer, or better defined as the disciples' prayer, introduces us to a new aspect of God. We see Him as a caring, tender Being who only wants the best for us. It is here that we come into contact with the very essence of His Fatherhood. This enables us, not only to understand Him in a new perspective, but also to be permitted to have a relationship with Him. Stop and think about this for a few minutes. God wants to have fellowship with each of us. Of all His names, both in the Old Testament and the New Testament, we finally come to the place where we find comfort and tenderness in His name, the name of Father. It is in the Gospel of John that the term "Father" is used 122 times. In each chapter of John's Gospel, there is a revelation of God as being a Father to His people. Again, this tells us a great deal about St. John as he took time to come to know His God as Father God. He knew Him to a point that He could actually feel the very heartbeat of God.

God, our Heavenly Father, yearns for each of us to come into that similar place of knowing Him. He wants us to feel His tenderness and love for all of His Creation. He wants each of His servants to feel His very own heartbeat. He is waiting for each of us to talk to Him so a relationship is finally established. Prayer is all about relationship.

There are numerous terms used in the New Testament, which begin with Father, such as: God the Father, God our Father, God and Father of our Lord Jesus Christ. All of these denote different aspects of His Fatherhood. It is through the person of Jesus Christ that we come to know God as our Father. In John 8:19, Jesus says, **"Then said they unto him, Where is thy Father?"** Jesus answered, *"Ye neither know me, nor my Father: if ye had known me, ye should have known my Father also."* Relationship with the Father is dependent upon first coming to know Jesus Christ as Lord and Savior. Only once in the New Testament did Jesus Christ deviate from calling God His Father. It is in Matthew 27:46, during Christ's agony on the cross when He calls to Him as **"My God."** *"And about the ninth hour Jesus cried with a loud voice saying, Eli, Eli, lama sabachthani? that is to say, My God, my God, why hast thou forsaken me?"* All other references to God are addressed as "Father."

When Jesus spoke the word "Father" not only did it express an eternal personal relationship, but also it set the scene for all believers to come into true intimacy with our Heavenly Father. Jesus had the most personal relationship with His loving Father. Christ is so certain of His Father's love for all those who had accepted His message, that He is able to say in John 10:28-30, **"Neither shall any man pluck them out of my hand...No man is able to pluck them out of my Father's hand. I and My Father are one."**

Coming into unity with the Father can only be accomplished as we yield ourselves to the Holy Spirit. God, our Father, wants all of His Creation to know Him in like manner. Of course, we will never be able to have such intimacy as Jesus Christ did with His Father. However, we will have our own intimacy with Him, which will be dependent upon our personal progressive sanctification. We are ever in the process of growing in holiness as we yield to the Holy Spirit. As we give up our own personal will to the Father, we will come to experience new intimacy and closeness with Him.

Things to consider:

God wants to have a personal relationship with me. <u>Do you want this</u>? Will you allow the Holy Spirit to draw you to your Heavenly Father's heart? His heart only purposes good for each of us. Isn't it time to stop doing your own thing and start seeking the God who loves you beyond your wildest imagination?

Pray something like this:

Dear Heavenly Father, please let me see You as a kind tender-hearted God. I want to know You intimately. Please help me. In His Precious name I pray. Amen.

God's Love for You

<u>My verse for today is</u>:
"**For with the heart man believeth unto righteousness; and with the mouth confession is made unto salvation**" (*Romans 10:10*).

Some time ago, my wife and I were blessed to see a miracle occur before our very own eyes. It was in the latter part of the seventies, that a lady came to a healing service where we were conducting our ministry. She had cancer in several parts of her body and had two major heart defects. This lady had recently returned from Henry Ford Hospital in Detroit, Michigan and had been told that she had only a little time left to live and should get her affairs in order. The lady came to our meeting believing that God would give her a miracle. She entered our prayer line, fell under the power of the Holy Spirit, and God totally healed her from cancer and heart disease. She lived another eighteen years and died in her eighties with great joy and anticipation of meeting our Lord Jesus Christ face to face.

This proved to me, beyond any shadow of a doubt, God's great care and concern for His children. Since this time, Rita and I have seen countless miracles attributed to God's devotion and love of His people. God is a God of absolute love, and God is a miracle worker! It is in Jesus Christ that we see the love of God so vividly displayed. Let us not forget that Jesus Christ is the second person of the Trinity or Godhead. Before His incarnation, Christ was in the form of God (Philippians 2:6-8). When He assumed manhood, He did not cease being God. His deity before the miraculous incarnation includes the fact that He could not cease being God. He was totally God and totally man. In becoming man, Jesus Christ displayed constant love and concern for all those around Him. His miracles, as well as His other great acts of love, illustrate His incredible love for His Creation. Jesus Christ can only love those that come to Him in faith.

In Hebrews 13:8, we read, **"Jesus Christ is the same yesterday, and to day, and for ever."** His character and love will never change for those who seek Him. Let us not forget that Jesus Christ was perfect love manifested for all mankind. He desires for each of us to know this love and to put it to practice loving others.

In the old Anglican Prayer Book, shortly before Communion, the Priest reminds believers, **"Thou shall love the Lord thy God with all thy heart, soul and mind. This is the first and great commandment and the second is like unto it. Thou shall love thy neighbor as thyself. On these two commandments hang all the Law and Prophets."** It is impossible for us to love God to this dimension, until we first realize how He loves us. We're the object of His love and adoration. When we come to know Christ Jesus as Lord and Savior, then we understand His profound love for us. This is a divine attribute of His holy deity. We read in 1 John 4:16: **"And we have known and believed the love that God hath to us. God is love; and he that dwelleth in love dwelleth in God, and God in him."**

The patriarchs of the Old Testament were given covenants of promise that the long awaited Messiah would come. They did not live to see that day, but we delight in knowing that Jesus Christ, out of His abundant love, came to bring all of us salvation if we so want it. Only the Son of God could give the world a fuller revelation of His Father. In the Old Testament, there was not a full revelation of God as a loving Father. Only fragmentary revelations were provided, and oftentimes they did not reveal the love nature of God. The revelation of God in the New Testament is that of a loving, tender Father. Jesus Christ gave us the clearest revelation of our Heavenly Father. Their relationship is representative of the relationship He wants to have with each of us. As we come into the new birth, by receiving Jesus Christ into our hearts by faith, a dynamic relationship then becomes possible.

Things to consider:

How do I receive Jesus Christ into my heart? What must I do to be saved? Jesus Christ came into the world to save all sinners, and I know that I have sinned. Will He really forgive me?

Take time to pray this prayer:

Lord Jesus Christ, You are the Son of God, and You have died for me and rose again. I confess that I need salvation since I am a sinner. Lord Jesus Christ, please come into my heart. Right now by faith, I receive You into my heart, into my soul, and into my spirit. By faith, I thank You for the gift of eternal life. I thank You that my sins are forgiven and that I am truly born-again.

God is a Good God

<u>My verse for today is</u>:
"And the Lord passed by before him, and proclaimed, The Lord, the Lord God, merciful and gracious, longsuffering, and abundant in goodness and truth" (Exodus 34:6).

There is no doubt in my mind about the goodness of God toward His Creation. He is constantly showing His love and concern for His children. The problem is we do not seem to recognize that He is all that is good. Many times we are dulled, or spiritually asleep, which disables us from recognizing the goodness of God. Do you ever take time to meditate about all the good things that have transpired in your life? Do you believe they just happened by chance or by divine planning?

We have often been told that God is love (1 John 4:17). Most have heard this truth since we were little children, but do we inwardly know/believe this in our spirit and soul? The answer is: Very few can truly see and recognize this attribute of God, but this still does not nullify His goodness. His goodness is often displayed in His providential care and concern for all of His Creation. We see this in Psalm 145:9, *"The Lord is good to all: and his tender mercies are over all his works."* In the New Testament, we again read of God's concern and care for His Creation. Matthew 6:26 says, *"Behold the fowls of the air: for they sow not, neither do they reap, nor gather into barns; yet your heavenly Father feedeth them. Are ye not much better than they?"*

There are numerous Scriptures, which talk about God and His goodness. Do we really take into consideration Christ's redemptive work on the cross? The Lord Jesus Christ died for all our sins, making complete and total atonement for all of humankind for all time. The Son of God, on behalf of those who truly did not deserve salvation, made this great and costly sacrifice. Upon His body, Jesus Christ took your sin and mine so that we could be a free people, enjoying a new relationship with the Father.

We see in Mel Gibson's film, *"The Passion of the Christ,"* the terrible physical agony that Jesus Christ suffered on the cross for all of mankind. However, do we ever consider the spiritual consequences of his crucifixion? Jesus Christ suffered spiritually far beyond our ability to imagine. He cried out, *"My God, My God, why hast thou forsaken me?"* (Mark 15:34). He was separated from God the Father as He endured our very own sins. Our finite reasoning faculties cannot comprehend Jesus' feeling of separation, loss and abandonment.

God sees our human condition and is moved with great compassion and sorrow as He beholds our miserable state. He desires to help all of us but is unable to do so because we do not turn to Him in prayer. Instead we close the door and wonder where God is in the midst of our human tragedy. God looks upon the human race with great mercy. We have drifted so far from God and His ways that a new awakening is necessary for mankind to get back on the right track.

Our human condition is the result of man's deliberate act of universal disobedience, yet God stands at the door of our human hearts and asks us to let Him in. Unfortunately we still do not acknowledge His immeasurable love and kindness that waits for those who accept Him. We see God's kindness as His gentle benevolence. In Psalm 31:21, *"Blessed be the Lord: for he hath shewed me his marvelous kindness in a strong city."* This is only one of numerous Scriptures that speaks of His love and kindness toward His Creation. God is a good God. Only those who take the time in prayer, and come into His presence, truly understand and comprehend this glorious truth.

God has provided the human race with His grace, which is often spoken about as His undeserved, unearned and unmerited favor. Take a moment and think about this aspect of His nature. It will overwhelm you after a time of reflection. Paul writes in Romans 2:4, *"Or despisest thou the riches of his goodness and forbearance and longsuffering; not knowing that the goodness of God leadeth thee to repentance?"*

Things to consider:

It is only as I seek our Lord Jesus Christ with all of my heart that I come to know the goodness of God. I must seek to form a partnership with God through Jesus Christ. My life must become a real partnership with Him, since He wishes to share in my joys and sorrows, triumphs, defeats, work and play. He wants to hold my hand day in and day out so I will never walk alone again. There is only one thing that will give real meaning to my Christian experience and that is union with Christ in humble and self-sacrificing love. To fail to achieve this is to let history pass me by. It is to miss the greatest force in this earthly life or even in the next, which is the infinite love of God and the knowledge of His goodness for all Creation.

Pray something like this:

Dear Heavenly Father, I want to know You and come into union with Jesus Christ. Lord, I know so little. Please lead me and guide me into total union with Your precious Son and the Holy Spirit. In His name I pray. Amen.

God is a Good God

God is Able

<u>My verse for today is</u>:
"But if any man love God, the same is known of him" (*1 Corinthians* 8:3).

What can God really do in your life? This is totally dependent upon your faith life. In our limited thinking, we curtail God's ability to work powerfully in our lives. At the same time, all things become possible with God if we trust in His ability to do for us what He wants and is needed to achieve His perfect will. Matthew 19:26 says, **"But Jesus beheld them, and said unto them, With men this is impossible; but with God all things are possible."** God is as big as our faith. He cannot supersede our faith level, unless others are praying on our behalf.

God's ability in you, and His innate ability, are two different things. Since God said, "Let there be light," this has never stopped. The universe is expanding at the rate of 186,000 miles per second. When is the universe going to stop? That will be when God Himself tells it to stop. His ability and His willingness to do for us what we pray for are dependent upon our relationship with Him. When I take the time on a daily basis to pray and seek Him, more of His ability will be released in my life. When I accept Jesus Christ as my Lord and Savior, I become a son of God. However, being a son of God means actively avoiding sin and its consequences. I must learn to stand before God without any sense of sin consciousness, and all feelings of inferiority must leave.

God craves to have fellowship with each one of us. It is in this new fellowship with the Father that I comprehend His ability on my behalf. Therefore all things do become possible. Our sonship is based upon our legal understanding of the New Birth. The knowing of Christ's great work at Calvary must become my reality. I am forgiven and cleansed in the blood of Jesus Christ and given my rightful place in the family of God. It is in this consciousness that I am given the nature of God Himself. The sin in my old nature is forced out by the life of Christ coming into my spirit. So, my spirit comes into perfect harmony with the Father. My spirit was recreated at the New Birth. Now all things become possible when I believe and take a stand for God. He becomes more than able to accomplish all things according to my faith level.

As we come to know the Holy Spirit, the third Person of the Trinity or Godhead, we comprehend God's profound ability and His ableness. When we are born-again, we are given the Holy Spirit, and when we are baptized in the Holy Spirit, at last He has us. This great gift of God brings two realities into our lives; the first is the New Life introducing us into the family of God and giving us a portion of His divine life.

The second is a New Presence, for the Divine Giver brings Himself along with His profound gift. We will never be alone again! When these things transpire in our lives, we not only consciously know that God is more than able, but we also come to learn He wants us to call upon His great power to perform the miraculous. We cannot see the Holy Spirit, but we possess Him in a more spiritual and intimate way. The Holy Spirit is sent to us on a mission of friendship, and He brings us to a place of knowing God's great ability on our own. He has been sent to indwell in us and to be our best friend. He is **"Christ in you, the hope of glory"** (Colossians 1:27b). Our Christian life will only mature as we come to know Him in prayer. He is the best friend you've always prayed for.

One cannot truly know God's ability until he/she comes into intimacy with the Almighty. Intimacy with God is not merely head knowledge but an actual experience of coming into a place in the Spirit where you experience God. This comes about as one seeks Him in prayer and the study of His Word. Worship and adoration are part of this procedure of coming into a spiritual acquaintance with God. Genesis 4:1 also says: **"And Adam knew Eve his wife; and she conceived, and bare Cain, and said, I have gotten a man from the Lord."** The word "know" in Hebrew is "yada" and it means to ascertain by seeing, acknowledge, discover, to experience, perceive, acquaintance, and it also implies to be one or fused together. The word "know" in the Greek is "ginosko" and seems to have almost the same meaning. It  means to be acquainted with a person, character, mind plans, to perceive (Mark 5:29), to understand, to discern, to distinguish, to get knowledge of.

Before one is able to say that "God is able," he has to come into a place of intimacy with the Lord. Thayer's Greek-English Lexicon of the New Testament further exegeses the word "to know" as becoming acquainted with, and is employed in the New Testament of the knowledge of God and Christ and the things relating to them or proceeding from them.[1][8] Only time, and a concerted effort in prayer, will bring us this knowledge of God's ability on our behalf. It is imperative that we take time to study the Bible, so we can see for ourselves how God has, through the centuries, spoken to man directly and indirectly.

Things to consider:

God wants to show Himself to me. He wants me to know that He can turn impossible situations around totally for the good. He wants me to understand that His power on my behalf is infinite. I must learn to trust and believe His Word and continually keep in prayer to see the hand of God move on my behalf.

Pray that you might come to know God in such an intimate way that all things will become possible in prayer. Ask the Lord to let you know of His ability on your behalf. Ask Him to show you that He is able in all things.

Pray something like this:

Dear Heavenly Father, I really want to know You! Help me overcome my finite limitations so I will truly believe You are more than able! I love You, Lord. Help me to grow spiritually so I might begin to feel Your very heartbeat. In Christ's name I pray. Amen.

Trusting God

<u>*My verse for today is*</u>:
"But let all those that put their trust in thee rejoice: let them ever shout for joy, because thou defendest them: let them also that love thy name be joyful in thee" *(Psalm 5:11).*

After many years of marriage, a man and a woman come to know each other in a most unique way. Many times they tell their friends and associates exactly what the other is thinking about at a particular time. They have come together in such a way that they perceive one another's feelings.

Trust is defined in the Concise Oxford Dictionary as a "firm belief in reliability, honesty, veracity, justice, strength, etc. of a person or thing." In other words, trust is a relationship with another, whereby we know beyond any shadow of a doubt, the character and nature of the person who is being trusted. Therefore, it is with our relationship with Almighty God where we come to that place of understanding and knowledge that God can never let us down.

In 2 Timothy 2:13 we read: *"If we believe not, yet he abideth faithful: he cannot deny himself."* You might say that this is the "Old Faithful One" who is always there when we need Him the most. It is this knowledge of His being that can cause us to trust the Lord without hesitation. But of course, this is going to take some time, and God will allow you to be tested in this matter. To know Him is to trust Him. How is this going to be achieved? It can only be accomplished through prayer with our Heavenly Father. It is going to require setting aside each day, either in the morning or evening, a specific time for prayer. It will require you to seek Him with all your heart, soul and spirit. Only in this manner of a personal pursuit will you ever get to know how trusting God will be to you. Deuteronomy 4:29 tells us, *"But if from thence thou shalt seek the Lord thy God, thou shalt find him, if thou seek him with all thy heart and with all thy soul."*

A trusting relationship with God, our Heavenly Father, begins the moment I call out to Him in prayer. He wants to show each of us that He can be found, but above all, that He can be trusted. Trust in the Almighty comes about as I get to personally know that He is there whenever I pray, and He never turns a deaf ear. As I begin to see answers to my prayers, I suddenly realize that He will answer me according to my faith. He has been there all the time, wanting me to pray and see Him move on my behalf.

Trusting God comes from knowing God. The degree to which I submit myself to the Holy Spirit will be the degree to which I can trust the Almighty. In other words, all talk without submission will not bring me into the position of truly trusting God. Obedience to our Lord is necessary if I am to come to know Him and trust in Him. It is through prayer and the yielding of my will to God the Father that allows my spiritual life to grow and helps me learn how to trust Him. When I was a young boy in Sunday school we sang, "Trust and obey, for there's no other way to be happy in Jesus, but to trust and obey." This sums up the entire issue. It is obedience that brings me to the place where I can trust the Lord.

__Things to consider:__

I can only come to a trusting relationship with God, our Heavenly Father, as I spend time in prayer getting to know Him. When I live in obedience, I learn to know and trust God. Knowing our Heavenly Father is the key to trusting Him. Prayer is something I must do every day to be able to achieve a knowing and trusting relationship with God.

__Pray something like this:__

Dear Heavenly Father, I come to You this day on bended knee because I want to know You and the power of Christ's resurrection. I want Your will in my life above all things. Help me to understand prayer, so that I might come into Your presence at any time. Help me to trust You. I ask this in Jesus' name. Amen.

Faith in God's Ability

My verse for today is:
"And Jesus said unto them, Because of your unbelief: for verily I say unto you, If ye have faith as a grain of mustard seed, ye shall say unto this mountain, Remove hence to yonder place; and it shall remove; and nothing shall be impossible unto you" *(Matthew 17:20)*.

Matthew 19:26 says, **"But Jesus beheld them, and said unto them, With men this is impossible; but with God all things are possible."** This statement found in Matthew's Gospel is truly beyond man's limited comprehension. The very reason some find this truth difficult to understand is that our "sense knowledge" has gained the upper hand in our educational and religious lives. This is the result of our constant contact with the physical world around us, and never taking into consideration that there is a greater world of the unseen.

We have learned to interpret the world around us through our five senses and have left out the Holy Spirit in so many things. Consequently, it is far easier to believe in the things that we see or even hear. It is imperative for us to comprehend that faith must be independent of our senses. When this begins to take place, we can then believe that all things are possible with God.

This incredible transition from the "sense realm" to the "spiritual realm" will not happen overnight. However, since it is based upon our prayer life, the more time, effort and energy spent on the frivolous things of life, the longer we will be held back from this dynamic realization of God's profound ability. Those who spend time in prayer and getting to know Him will soon realize our God and the total ability that exists in Him.

We must not forget that the Bible demands faith in things that our natural senses cannot understand. God's ability is one of those things that must be understood in terms of faith in God and His Word. Hebrews 11:3 tells us that the world has been formed by faith through the spoken Word of God. ***"Through faith we understand that the worlds were framed by the word of God, so that things which are seen were not made of things which do appear."*** All things are possible to those who have faith and put their trust in God. Countless times in our ministry, we have seen miracles occur right before our eyes. Seemingly impossible situations have been turned around as we have concentrated our efforts in prayer. Consequently, we believe that all things are possible with God, but there is one stipulation and that is our faith. Do you personally believe that all things are possible with God? God's ability is limited only according to our faith.

Hebrews 11:1 says, ***"Now faith is the substance of things hoped for, the evidence of things not seen."*** Literally, faith is giving substance to things hoped for. When God said, "Let there be light," it has never stopped since. His ability is limitless! We all need to grasp this truth; His ability toward us is also limitless.

In Mark 9:23, we read: ***"In thou canst believe, all things are possible to him that believeth."*** Again, this is another Scripture verse that challenges us personally. God's ability is not dependent upon us, rather it is dependent upon our faith. Do I have what it takes to see and believe the impossible? 1 John 4:4b says, ***"Greater is he that is in you, than he that is in the world."*** If I am truly born again, then God's Spirit dwells within me. Therefore, His ability is able to do for me all that my faith is able to believe.

Through history, God's ability was expressed in the life of Martin Luther as well as in the ministry of John Alexander Dowie with so many miraculous healings. He witnessed new eyes given after the original had been surgically removed. Through many years of ministry I, too, have seen God's ability in individuals who have closely linked themselves to God. Above all, God's ability is vividly clear in the ministry of Jesus Christ. With words that He spoke, He even quieted the sea when He said, *"Peace, be still"* (Mark 4:35-39).

In Acts 3:6, we see Peter's faith in action by the use of the Savior's name. We read, *"Then Peter said, Silver and gold have I none; but such as I have give I thee: In the name of Jesus Christ of Nazareth rise up and walk."* Faith in God's ability will grow as we learn to pray and seek His face. Prayer and Bible study on a daily basis brings a greater trust in God's ability since it is in God's Word that we discover the limitless ability of God. We see Him as He really is — a God who loves His Creation and would do for them all that they ask of Him. We need to develop a relationship with Him through Jesus and the Holy Spirit and then have the faith and willingness to ask.

One of the greatest miracles ever recorded in the Bible is that of Sarah and Abraham. God gave them a son after Sarah's womb had been unfruitful for nearly ninety years. Romans 4:19-20 is a commentary on Abraham's faith. Here we read, *"And being not weak in faith, he considered not his own body now dead, when he was about an hundred years old, neither yet the deadness of Sarah's womb; He staggered not at the promise of God through unbelief; but was strong in faith, giving glory to God, and being fully persuaded that, what he had promised, he was able also to perform."* God's ability on our behalf is shown to those who fear not. It is shown to those who take a step in faith. None of us will ever know God's enormous ability until we take tiny steps of faith by doing what He has asked us to do. Faith is the key that will unleash God's ability on behalf of the believer.

Things to consider:

People of faith, who have been challenged to believe in the impossible, will see God's ability. As I walk on this pilgrimage, challenges will come that will cause me to believe for God's ability on my behalf. Seemingly impossible events and circumstances will be altered as I take the time to seek the Lord in prayer. My prayer life will determine the degree to which I see God's ability demonstrated. Prayer must become a daily event for which I long to do.

Pray something like this:

My Lord and my God, You are everything to me. Please help me see Your ability in my own life. Let my faith grow each and every time I read Your Word and pray to seek You. Lord, so much of this is really new to me, and I need Your Spirit to guide me along this pilgrim path. Help me to grow in faith and trust of You. I ask this in the infallible name of Jesus Christ. Amen.

The Infallible Word

<u>My verse for today is</u>:
"All scripture is given by inspiration of God, and is profitable for doctrine, for reproof, for correction, for instruction in righteousness" *(2 Timothy 3:16)*.

"I judge that my prayer is more than the devil himself; if it were otherwise, Luther would have fared differently long before this. Ye men will not see and acknowledge that great wonders or miracles God works in my behalf. If I should neglect prayer but a single day, I should lose a great deal of the fire of faith." Martin Luther[1] [9]

It is virtually impossible to have a successful prayer life until one comes to grips with the issue of the Bible. What does the Bible mean to you? Is it just a nice book filled with fables, myths and legends or is it the mind of God speaking to us? This is a question that you will have to answer if you want to see results in your prayer life.

Martin Luther, one of the great church reformers, knew the power of God's Word. It almost cost him his life. He made up his mind that the Bible was truly God's Word. It was the mind of God being expressed to us in written form. He believed the Bible was totally inspired by the Spirit of God, and no man was capable of such matchless insight. It was God speaking to His Creation on the pages of inspired manuscripts. However, what does the Bible mean to you?

Until you answer this question, all else concerning your prayer life is virtually worthless. We need to know God's Word to pray effectively. It is the knowledge and basic understanding of God's Word that changes an ordinary life into an extraordinary life. It means the difference of a spiritual life of mediocrity or excellence. Multitudes have died in defense of God's Word. Wars have been fought during the Middle Ages over acquisition of God's Word. It is truly inspired by the Holy Spirit, and that is why it has been such an offense to countless multitudes through the ages. These were the individuals who refused to accept the fact that God spoke through His prophets and chosen ones in His Word. God's thoughts are known unto those who will faithfully read His Book.

Martin Luther was not only an orator of God's Word but also a man of great prayer. He knew how to get a hold of God during the most desperate of times. If he couldn't have prayed, I'm sure he would've died from trepidation and fear. Not many people have gone through what he experienced while trying to bring a message of faith through God's Word to the multitudes.

The Word of God is a road map to learn the different ways of praying, but most of all, it is to be used to help us to be effective in our praying. God's Word is the guide that will unlock the impossible as we come to the knowledge that what is expressed in the Bible can become an actuality. All things become possible if one will take the time to appreciate the integrity of God's Word.

That which has been accomplished in the past in the Spirit can be repeated in the present even to a greater measure. This was our Lord's perspective when He said: **"Verily, verily, I say unto you, He that believeth on me, the works that I do shall he do also; and greater works than these shall he do; because I go unto** *my Father"* (John 14:12). Men of prayer have not exhausted the past. The modern day church must not be dependent on yesterday's miracles, but must through prayer, seek a new day of miracles. The church that is constantly looking to yesterday is a church that is not in touch with the Holy Spirit. We need a new day of the miraculous, which can only come to us because someone is not frightened to believe the Word of God. It is faith in God's Word, coupled with diligent prayer, that will bring about vast spiritual change to not only our nation but also the world.

God is looking for a people who will take Him at His Word. He is looking for men and women who want to do the will of God above all things. He is seeking out men and women who have turned their hearts entirely toward God. Such people will actualize their prayers even to a greater realization than those saints of the past.

Things to consider:

The Bible is God's infallible Word. It is the mind of God being expressed to me through the power of the Holy Spirit, as He moved upon men of old to write it. It is eternal; nothing will ever change the Word of God in spite of what man, or the devil, may have conspired to do.

Pray something like this:

Oh, Eternal Heavenly Father, I come to You this day in faith believing all that Your Word has to tell me. Please give me the grace and strength to love and appreciate Your infallible Word. Let me see it come to pass as I pray according to Your Word. I give You the praise and the glory since You hear me as I pray. In Jesus' name, I do pray. Amen.

Seeking God

<u>My verse for today is</u>:
"And all the angels stood round about the throne, and about the elders and the four beasts, and fell before the throne on their faces, and worshipped God" (Revelation 7:11).

"**When thou saidst, Seek ye my face; my heart said unto thee, Thy face, Lord, will I seek**" (Psalm 27:8). There is within every living human, an inordinate spiritual vacuum that haunts us until the day we are found by God. There is an eternal quest within every human being to know God and His truth. Some will take their whole lives in pursuit of things, never coming to the knowledge that it is God who is trying to get their attention.

At times, man seems to go crazy for awhile, until he finds the truth of God's existence and His great love for His Creation. Some will try drugs, alcohol, sex and a host of other things rather than finding the reality of the Almighty. How do I know this? Because I myself tried many things until I was found by the Lord.

Seeking God is so very important in each of our lives. We all must come to the knowledge of the Eternal One. God's endless pursuit is for us to come into relationship with Him. Without a relationship with our Heavenly Father, there can be no real sonship. This would not satisfy the heart of our Father, nor would it ever satisfy us. Fellowship is only possible through Jesus Christ and His selfless sacrifice that took place at Calvary. We are able to go into God's presence at any time, knowing that He will listen and will answer us according to His divine will.

Prayer is one of the greatest ways of seeking God. Prayer opens God's ears to our hearts' cries. Seeking God brings an inward change to each individual. Seeking God is not a religious activity, but it is rather being still and letting Him lead and guide us into greater truth. It's about holding His hand and listening to Him. We can do all kinds of spiritual good works but still not grow in the Spirit or ever come to that place of really knowing God.

We need to resign ourselves from the cult of religious activity and just seek God in prayer. If we do this, there will come a new enlightened knowledge of God and His goodness toward His Creation. Many people, with a sincere effort to seek God, will pray and fast more, as well as engage in more Bible study. After a maximum effort of doing all kinds of religious activities, they will give up their efforts, believing He must not be there for them. Let us remember, this is not the way to seek the Lord, but man's way of doing things. God will manifest Himself to those who seek Him when they cease from the cult of religious commotion.

It is learning to walk in the Spirit that will open the doors of finding God and lead to a deeper knowledge of Christ. Walking in the Spirit allows God to do in us what He desires to do. It may be an insightful change in our inner person, which then allows us not to seek God, but to find Him in a new way. Walking and living in the Spirit will never come to an end since we will constantly want more of God.

Seeking God is a lifelong process; it only ends when God takes us out of our bodies to Heaven. This process is one of self-crucifixion so God might manifest Christ in us to the world. As we come into a greater knowledge of God, we realize we must yield to the Spirit if we are to come to truly know Him.

If there was one thing in the life of Jesus Christ, which characterized His life from all others, it was His unconditional submission to the Spirit of His Heavenly Father. Jesus said, *"...I do nothing of myself; but as my Father hath taught me, I speak these things...for I do always those things that please him"* (John 8:28-29).

It has been said that the Spirit, which was in Christ, was not given in measure, but to each of us we have a measure of the Spirit. It is our willingness to yield to the Holy Spirit that will enable us to know the Spirit in His fullness. Many never understand the purpose of the Holy Spirit in their lives. We must understand that the Spirit is given to us to become like Christ. This teaching is very much needed in the Church today. In other words, seeking God means dying to self and becoming alive in Christ. The degree to which you yield yourself to the Holy Spirit will be the degree to which you find God Almighty.

Seeking God means dying to self and wanting to become like Christ. True yieldedness to Christ means that every thought, word, deed, and purpose in life is to willingly bring all things to Him, and seek the direction and control of the Holy Spirit. When we completely desire and want to know and find God, it will mean our own trip to Calvary for self-crucifixion. The human being does not like to "submit" to the Lordship of Jesus Christ. Most of us fear that we will lose our own will. This is just not so! Giving up our will to God allows Him to do His work in us, and this will allow us to be used of God. Our purpose in life will be fulfilled.

True yielding to the Spirit requires nothing of you. It is an attitude, not only of the heart, but also of the mind. Yieldedness to the Spirit is a passive state of mind. There is no resistance on our part; we allow the Holy Spirit the right to do what He so desires in us. How is this accomplished? We simply must not resist the Spirit when He is attempting to teach us, guide us, correct us or discipline us. The Spirit may lead us into a situation that will cause our flesh to suffer anguish even though we would want to solve the problem ourselves.

Only the Spirit can bring about a resolution to a trial or difficulty. He will root out all kinds of denominational doctrines and even the traditions of men. We may have held onto these various things for years, but soon they fall to the wayside. We change and become a transformed individual in Christ. The result of seeking God in this exciting new way is to come into a new spiritual dimension. It is impossible for me to explain exactly what new dimension of the Spirit you might come into, but I can guarantee you will arrive safely! Be assured God has everything under His control.

There is a poem by Rabidranath Tagore, a Benedictine monk of the last century, which helps put things in true perspective.

"Day after day, O Lord of my life,
Shall I stand before Thee, face to face.
With folded hands, O Lord of all worlds,
Shall I stand before Thee, face to face.
Under the great sky, in solitude and
Silence, with humble heart,
Shall I stand before Thee, face to face."

This monk had come to the final conclusion before his death, that following the Spirit means doing nothing. It was allowing the Holy Spirit in us to do what He desires so that we finally come to that glorious place of finding God. The poem deals with the finality of life and the realization of the Eternal. It is a journey that all of us will make, but it begins in seeking God one step at a time. The journey ends when we stand before God on the day we leave these bodies for our eternal endless home with Christ.

The Holy Spirit initiates seeking God, and the finality of our journey ends with the knowledge of the Holy. Seeking never really comes to an end in this life. When you learn one thing about God, you will always want more. It is this priceless knowledge of our Holy Lord that brings a soul into union with Christ.

Things to consider:

Seeking God is a never-ending journey that begins the moment I realize how empty I am without His presence in my life. I will find out truths about God, but they will satisfy me for just a short time since I will always want to know more. I am on a pilgrim journey in this life, and it can only end when I have attained all that He wants me to grasp. One day I will see Him face to face. It is then that my journey will have been fulfilled in the knowledge of the Holy. Daily prayer is essential if I am to come into that place where I begin to see God as He is. I must understand that it is prayer on a routine basis that is going to advance my journey. Seeking God begins on my knees and ends with my hands lifted up unto the Holy One.

Pray something like this:

Dear Heavenly Father, please take my hand and lead me on my pilgrim journey toward Heaven. Oh God, let every day be filled with more knowledge of You. In Christ's name.

Abiding In Him

<u>My verse for today is</u>:
"**Herein is my Father glorified, that ye bear much fruit; so shall ye be my disciples**" (John 15:8).

"Abide in me, and I in you. As the branch cannot bear fruit of itself, except it abide in the vine; no more can ye, except ye abide in me" (John 15:4). Here in this verse we begin to see what is being asked of each of us. The Greek, "meno" means to remain, continue, dwell and abide. This is a command given to us so we might bear fruit for our Lord. It is a state of being in Christ where the saint only wants what the Lord desires of him. Prayer can only achieve this particular state in the Spirit. It is coming to know Jesus Christ in prayer that gives us the desire to occupy our self with Him. It is in this manner that the saints can bear the fruit of the Holy Spirit. We are all called to be fruit bearers. Unfortunately, many of us bear very little fruit because we do not take sufficient time in prayer.

There are many great lessons we can learn from the Bible in John chapter 15. First, God is the husbandman (verse 1). Christ is the vine (verse 1 and 5). Believers are the branches in Christ. Since we are in Christ, it is expected that we might bear fruit. Those branches that don't bear fruit are cut off, withered, gathered with other dead branches and cast into the fire and burned (verse 2 and 6). Every branch "in me" is purged that it might become more fruitful (verse 2 and 5).

That being said, it is not uncommon for Christians to go through very difficult times. Have you recently undergone some tough times, and you cannot explain why you had to experience such a time? You were being purged so that you might bear fruit. Not everything in the Christian life is always the way we want it to be. There are times when you will seek God in prayer just to change your circumstances. Prayer is the spiritual instrument that allows us to rid ourselves of the burdens that so easily come upon us.

There is only one precise reason why we as Christians suffer; it is to bear the fruit of the Spirit. We are made to be peculiar people who manifest Christ to the world. This can only happen as we occupy ourselves with Christ and the things of God. We are the branches that appear in John 15, and we must "abide in" Christ if we are to produce real fruit. In and of ourselves, we are incapable of bearing fruit. It is through prayer and meditation upon Christ that we can begin to produce the qualities of character that resemble those of our Lord.

Christ Himself is incapable of producing fruit in our lives unless we take every opportunity to abide in Him. The branches must abide (or remain) in Him for nurture and support. Unless we abide in Him, we may be cut off and burned (v. 6). Not only must we abide in Him, but we also need to have His Word in us, or we will spiritually dry up. This is a terrible condition when we as saints lack His Word in us. It is like a beautiful plant that blossoms and blooms but then is deprived of water. The plant will soon die from dehydration.

As we learn to abide in Christ, the branches glorify God. While we remain in Christ and produce fruit, we become totally different people, showing the world the presence of the indwelling Christ. We soon learn that apart from Christ, we are nothing. This is because naturally, God never intended that we should "be apart" from Him. We were created from nothingness, yet we were created in His image.

Through the blood of Jesus Christ, we were molded in the likeness of Himself. *Prayer is the glorious means by which we attain true spirituality by the power of His Holy Spirit.* As we occupy ourselves in Christ, we begin to see clearly our native state of complete dependence upon God, and then to gratefully accept this revelation with total peace of mind.

Occupying ourselves with Christ does not give us the time to be worried over past mistakes or sins. It is now time that we go with God into greater realms of the Spirit. When we occupy ourselves with Christ, we realize that self-sufficiency is a naïve attitude. Our sufficiency is in knowing Christ and the power of His resurrection. As we come to this place in Christ, we understand that our personal success is really another gift from God. Abiding in Christ creates a completely new mindset.

As we study our desires, we begin to have a personal knowledge of ourselves. Does my heart really seek to abide in Christ? Your desires are a dead giveaway of what is taking place in your spirit. Desire might be compared to a thermometer that actually measures our spiritual lives. Is Christ all that I want or desire? Sensual desires create a sensual person. When we are self-centered, we create a mediocre and selfish life. It is only when our sight is focused on Christ that our lives begin to make true spiritual progress of "abiding in Him."

Once again, it is time to awaken our souls for our need of God and His Holy Spirit. It is in this way we will not be a burden to ourselves or those around us; instead we will be a blessing. This will be accomplished as we occupy ourselves with the things of the Kingdom. Jesus Christ desires that we come into the place where our lives are in tune with His Holy Spirit. Every aspect of your life will be enriched so everything you do will be like a symphony orchestra, playing totally in tune with the concert music under the direction of Jesus Christ.

Abiding in Christ brings true freedom to the soul; it is through this completely new lifestyle that we will find peace, power, and purpose for our existence. As we occupy ourselves with Jesus Christ and His Word, we will have the distinct ability to discern. We will know what is of God and what is not of God. We will not be ignorant of satan's devices, since we will be occupied with the things of God's Spirit. At no other time is our need for discernment as vitally important as it is today.

Our world is in great need of a spiritual awakening as the forces of hell are being mustered against the Church. It is in prayer, as our lives are being totally given to our Lord, that we will see great victories in the lives of those around us. It is total occupation with Jesus Christ and His Word that can bring change to friends, families, entire communities and ourselves.

Abiding in Him by the power of prayer ignites the fire of God's love within us. Personal revival is the end product of prayer that brings about the desire of seeing others brought into the Kingdom. *It is prayer that will cause multitudes of people to come into the Kingdom of God.* Occupying ourselves with Christ will bring a spiritual move of God in our lives and others that can affect the entire world. It is time that we make up our minds to abide in Christ in a completely new dimension. Yesterday's anointing is not sufficient for today. It is in abiding in Christ that a daily fresh anointing of God's Spirit will come upon each of us.

As we abide in Christ, we soon realize that we have personal character limitations that God wants to correct. A famous author once said that the first step in character formation is to know what the worst in us is. This is probably the point in our character that the devil constantly probes, looking to gain a foothold. To be successful against satan, we need to be well aware of our character weaknesses. As you occupy yourself with Christ, you will soon learn your chief weakness is the principal character defect in our personalities. It is a kind of spiritual allergy to a certain fond sin or even vice. It constantly infiltrates our way of thinking and behaving towards others and ourselves.

In the life of St. Augustine, he once prayed: "O Lord, that I may know Thee; That I may know myself." St. Augustine had been a very sensual man before coming to Christ. He did understand that occupying our self with Christ would bring that precious balance of the knowledge of God with the knowledge of one's self. St. Augustine did face up to his faults, especially sensuality. As he continued to occupy himself with Christ, he truly resolved to combat his besetting sin. At the end of his life, he could truthfully say that it was Jesus Christ and His Spirit that gave him the victory over his sin.

Things to consider:

When I make up my mind to truly occupy myself with Christ and the things of His Kingdom, it is then that I will have the knowledge and joy of knowing Him by the power of His Spirit. I can never be truly happy as a Christian until I make this commitment of giving myself whole-heartedly to Christ. It is with such a commitment that I will hear His Spirit speak within my soul. The leading, teaching, and discernment of God's Spirit will not be a thing to grasp but a reality in my life.

Pray something like this:

Dear Lord Jesus, I want to occupy myself totally with You. It is in this realization that I will be truly happy. Anything less than all of You is to my spiritual detriment. I abandon myself to Your will and purpose for my life. Send Your Spirit of Grace upon me so that I might constantly delight myself in Your glorious presence. In Christ's holy name. Amen.

The Reverence of God

My verse for today is:
"Ye shall be holy; for I the Lord your God am holy" *(Leviticus 19:2).*

Have you ever taken the time to ask yourself just how you feel about God? In what capacity do you look to Him? Is He Lord of your life or just someone you occasionally talk to?

It is imperative to understand that we serve a Holy God, and we are a part of His vast Creation. We are the expression of the mind of God, and the entire purpose of our Creation was to come not only to know God, but come into that place of intimacy of worship. Consequently, we must see God as a being that we should hold much reverence for. He is the Creator, and we are His Creation.

In Hebrews 12:29, we get some idea of God's nature. *"**For our God is a consuming fire.**"* This refers to the holiness of God's character or nature. He is a Holy God, Who is deserving of our total reverence. Let us comprehend that fire is not God, but He

Himself is described as a consuming fire. Again, this goes back to a basic definition of God and understanding that He is light. Fire is the most common symbol of God used in the Bible. It is used on numerous occasions to signify His holiness and absolute righteousness that is manifested in judgment against man's sin.

Since God is holy, it becomes proper that we, who are His Creation, should revere God for the being that He is. If we would just take a good look around this world, we would be awestruck at God's brilliance in His Creation. Man does not have the intelligence or wisdom to create life as God has done. The human being is perhaps the most complex of all Creation. Still, we cannot even begin to create life. To think that we are the creation of slime from the ocean's floor is not to think at all; only a most comprehensive Being could have created us.

During the Twentieth Century, there was a move away from showing reverence towards God and the things of God. Nowadays our young people have little reverence, if any, towards God. This is one thing that must be taught over and over to those who desire a greater relationship with God.

When we speak of the attributes of God, we speak of qualities or characteristics, which belong only to Him. It is His attributes that make God Who He is. This distinguishes humankind from all that is God. We are the Creation, and He is the infinite Creator.

God's holiness implies the quality of absolute purity. Not even for a second will our God tolerate any kind of sin. In theology, He is known as Sinless Perfection. Holiness is God's inner being, and as such, it is the basis for foundation. Whatever He thinks, says, or does is an act of perfect holiness. It has been implied by the Ancient Church that holiness is the ability to exist in consistence with the nature of God's life.

There are numerous Scriptural passages that reference God's holiness. **"Ye shall be holy, for I the Lord your God am holy"** (Leviticus 19:2). Again in Exodus 15:11, **"Who is like thee, glorious in holiness."** Even in the Book of Isaiah 57:15 we read, **"For** *thus saith the high and lofty One that inhabiteth eternity, whose name is Holy."* There are many references in the Bible concerning the nature of God's holiness. This alone should induce reverence in His Creation.

As we take the time to pray and seek God in His Word, we will develop an understanding and reverence for the Being He actually is. We must become enlightened in our prayers to realize that we can ask God only for what He wants us to ask of Him; He wills only what is conformable to His divine will. Our prayer, therefore, must become "ordered"; in other words, our prayers must be consistent with the order of God Himself.

Much of our praying should be centered on knowing our Holy God, Who is worthy of all praise and reverence. God is our Alpha and Omega, the Beginning and the End. As we pray, He becomes the light of our minds and the strength of our wills. He is the summation of all truth, goodness and beauty, and He is the stream or source of all joy. He  is the source of all life. How we need to revere our God! Therefore, in our prayer, we must come to that place where we ask God for Himself. We must become united with Him, to be transformed and to be possessed totally by His Holy Spirit. As we begin to see God in the light of His holiness, we too, will want to become holy.

Prayer is that force which opens our spirits to the light of the nature of God. Prayer then becomes an instrument to help us along the pilgrim path of holiness. Nothing less than this will satisfy our souls. The more time you spend with the Lord in prayer, the more it will cause a deep inner conviction that you, too, must become more like Him. Contentment will never be found in this life unless we seek to be like our God. The love of money, luxury, or sex cannot bring to the soul the inner harmony and peace needed to survive this life here on earth.

Reverence for God must be based on the knowledge of His holiness; if not, reverence for Him will always be arbitrary. It is through prayer that we gain the perfect vision of His being, and it brings true joy to any man who will seek it out. As we take the time to make a total gift of our lives, He responds by giving Himself as a total gift to our spirits. Prayer brings one into unity with God so that a holy reverence for His being can become part of our actuality. God is to be reverenced, since He is Perfect Holiness.

Things to be considered:

God is Perfect Holiness, worthy of all my reverence. He cannot tolerate sin in any form. His nature, through Jesus Christ, can become part of the New Birth experience in Christ. I must seek Him in prayer so that I might become one with His infinite being.

Pray something like this:

Dear Heavenly Father, You are Perfect Holiness, and I totally revere You for the kind and loving Father that You are. Help me to understand You better as the person You are and above all, help me to become more like You. In Christ's name I do pray. Amen.

Heart, Mind and Soul

<u>My verse for today is</u>:
"And the very God of peace sanctify you wholly; and I pray God your whole spirit and soul and body be preserved blameless unto the coming of our Lord Jesus Christ" *(1 Thessalonians 5:23).*

There are a few things we need to understand about man before we discuss this chapter heading. First, man owes his existence to Almighty God who created him from the beginning. Consequently, this makes man a dependent creature. Man is not self-existent and never will be independent of God. Each and every breath that man takes is totally dependent upon God. We find in Acts 17:23-31 that *"in him we live, and move, and have our being."* It is in God that all of this transpires.

God created man to have emotions, which we know are expressed every day in each of us. Man is created as a tripartite being. We are spirit, soul and body. Man is a human spirit; the part of him which will live forever is called his spirit (pneuma). This is the God-conscious part of a human being since his spirit is capable of knowing God.

When man was created, God formed the spirit of man within man himself; *"and formeth the spirit of man within him"* (Zechariah 12:1b). Now we begin to see that God is the God of all spirits (Numbers 16:22). It is man's spirit that is able to worship God who desires that we worship in spirit.[1][10] In Proverbs 20:27, the Bible says, *"The spirit of man is the candle of the Lord, searching all the inward parts of the belly."* The spirit has intuition or conscience and is able to have communion with God and others.

In the Bible, the soul (psueche) is considered to be the self-conscious part of man. The soul is capable of knowing one's self. Earlier in our study, we saw in the Creation account God forming man's body from the dust of the earth, that He breathed into man *"the breath of life,"* or more correctly, put in *"the breath of lives"* (Genesis 2:7). It is as God first breathed into man's body that he received his spirit and soul. The apostle Paul tells us in 1 Corinthians 15:45-47 that man became a living soul. In theology, the soul is considered to be the central part of man, which connects both spirit and body in its unity. The soul has the power of influencing both the spirit and the body because of its centrality. It is said to have the human faculties of mind, will and emotions.

The body (soma) is the part of us that is seen by those around us. Bodies come in all sizes and dimensions and are subject to their environments. The spirit, soul and body are significant of the totality of man or his whole personality.[2][11] We see this in 1 Thessalonians 5:23, *"And the very God of peace sanctify you wholly; and I pray God your whole spirit and soul and body be preserved blameless unto the coming of our Lord Jesus Christ."*

The heart (kardia) in the New Testament is considered to be the seat of reason and the will as well as the emotions.[3][12] In 1 Peter 3:4, the heart is referred to as the inner man. The heart in the New Testament is above all the central place in man to which God turns to get our attention.

In the Old Testament, the word "heart" is seen in 1 Samuel 9:20 as mind. *"And as for thine asses that were lost three days ago, set not thy mind on them; for they are found. And on whom is all the desire of Israel? Is it not on thee, and on thy father's house?"* At times the word "heart" is used in place of mind, but it means the same thing.

So, the heart, mind and soul are very important to us in seeking and knowing God. Prayer is the means by which perfect unity occurs in man as he seeks God with his heart, mind and soul. We are exhorted to love God with all our heart, mind and soul. This is done as we begin to worship God with all of our energy and personal strength. We see this clearly in Revelation 22:8 as John was shown powerful things in the spirit. He fell prostrate before the feet of the angel who showed him these things.

John's intention was to worship this messenger of the Lord. But the messenger said, **"...Refrain! You must not do that. I am (only) a fellow servant along with yourself and of your brethren the prophets, and of those who are mindful and practice (the truths contained in) the messages of this book. Worship God!"** (v. 9, the Amplified Bible). God alone is worthy to receive such praise and adoration.

"So they left the tomb hastily with fear and great joy, and ran to tell the disciples. And as they went, behold, Jesus met them and said, Hail (greeting)! And they went up to Him and clasped His feet and worshipped Him" (Matthew 28:8-9, Amplified Bible). Verses 17-20 describe what happened when Jesus' disciples saw their resurrected Lord. **"And when they saw Him they fell down and worshipped Him, but some doubted. Jesus approached and breaking the silence said to them, All authority - all power of rule - in heaven and on earth has been given to Me. Go then and make disciples of all the nations, baptizing them into the name of the Father and of the Son and of the Holy Spirit; Teaching them to observe everything that I have commanded you, and lo, I am with you all the days, - perpetually, uniformly and on every occasion - to the (very) close and consummation of the age. Amen – so let it be"** (Matthew 28:17-20, Amplified Bible).

The Bible is full of examples of people prostrating themselves as an act of worship. This manner of worship speaks of great humility and submission to our Lord Jesus Christ. We see the mind, soul and spirit all involved in this intense form of worship. At the same time, this can be considered a special kind of prayer. The Greek word "proskuneo" conveys this manner of prayer and worship. It is used to describe the act of worship as one "prostrates himself in reverence to pay homage." This is an outward act of worship, and it speaks of an outward (physical or body) act of worship. Many people will prostrate themselves in humility and submission to the Almighty. Oftentimes it will occur in deep prayer. The heart, mind and soul are engrossed with the love of God. This kind of prayer can really move mountains.

It is in such determined prayer that God hears and will readily answer His servant. This prayer is directed by the Holy Spirit and does not occur very often. When it does take place, the servant can rest assured that God has heard and will readily answer him.

Things to consider:

When I fervently seek God with my heart, mind and soul, it is then that I am truly worshipping and seeking God in prayer. When I lay prostrate before God, it shows an act of great humility and submission.

Pray something like this:

Dear Heavenly Father, I want my mind, heart and soul to be totally involved as I seek You. Please give me the grace and wisdom so that I might pray just like that. I truly want to pray with my entire being. In Christ's name. Amen.

How to Love God

<u>My verse for today is</u>:
"And this they did, not as we hoped, but first gave their own selves to the Lord, and unto us by the will of God" *(2 Corinthians 8:5)*.

When we consider God's great love for us, and how He gave up His only begotten Son as a human sacrifice to make atonement for all the sins of mankind, the only response possible is that we love Him.

At times it may appear that the dealings of God toward His Creation are somewhat harsh. As we begin to see through things that come against us, we then realize the goodness of God. Problems that come our way are not sent to hurt or harm us, but to draw us nearer to our loving Heavenly Father.

Prayer is conversing with our tender loving Father. Some find it difficult to pray because they have an exaggerated notion of prayer; they don't really understand what it means and erroneously believe that it consists of lofty thoughts and words. This is not true. Take for example the thoughts and words of the Centurion, the leper, the blind man, and others mentioned in the Gospels who sought help from our Lord and were heard! With every word uttered to Him, He takes the time to listen and respond. Not all answers to prayer are what we might want to receive, but it behooves us to understand that God always gives us the best answers.

Our prayers are like incense ascending before the throne of God, or a golden key, which unlocks the treasures of heaven. God's love is continuously emitted to the saint who prays. We meet with our God in our secret place, just to find out that He is waiting for us to love Him once again. Take time to think about all the good things that have come your way. A wonderful wife or husband, a good job, a new car, a lovely home, and good friends - do you think these things just happen? Is it possible that perhaps God might have had something to do with it?

I once knew a wonderful elderly Episcopal priest by the name of Father Frank Dearing. In his book, About God and People, he makes this statement: "It says that most high God, Creator of all universes, cared so much about one little species of one creature on one little planet that He came and joined them and become one of them."[1] [13] When we consider the person of Jesus Christ, His life, His death, and His resurrection, there is virtually nothing more to say about how much God our Father loves us.

The apostle Paul said, **"For the preaching of the cross is to them that perish foolishness; but unto us which are saved it is the power of God"** (1 Corinthians 1:18). The greatest thing people can know is that God really loves them. This profound and unselfish love can be found in prayer on a daily basis. Prayer is the vehicle that brings the love of God to all of His Creation.

Going back to Father Frank Dearing, he says in his book, "It was that God the Son, became completely man, loved with such joyful power that the minds, and souls, and bodies of the people who touched Him were changed into something new." It is the very same today. As we pray, we touch the heart of God, and all the shackles of self-made bondages are broken forever.

God cares, and above all, God loves His fallen Creation. How far will love go in seeking out the lost? The answer is quite simple — as far as it is necessary to find one lost sinner. He will set you up for salvation. This is one of the reasons I call God the "Great Setter-Upper." He does all that is needed by His infinite grace to save even one lost sinner.

In her book, <u>Children and Religion</u>, Dora Chaplain says, "Experience shows that many little children whose religious life unfolds naturally seem to have, in some unfathomable way, a perception through which the character of Jesus is already half-knowledge: as though, when you teach, you are only introducing two dear friends already known to each other. Many parents testify of this experience."[2] [14]

It is in the quiet of the prayer closet the "two friends" finally come to the place that each knows of the sublime love that exists between them. But if there is never an initial encounter between God and man, there can only exist confusion. When one is found of God through prayer, the love relationship between them becomes ecstatic. It is my opinion that finding the love of God is the most important act in all of His Creation. When we realize His enormous care and love for His Creation, there are not enough words in our limited language to describe this glorious truth.

Could we not say that prayer is love shared between those who make the prayers and the One Who answers them? As we learn these prayer truths, a whole new world opens up to each of us. Paul says in 2 Corinthians 5:17, **"Therefore if any man be in Christ, he is a new creature: old things are passed away; behold, all things are become new."** Love has the ability to totally transform the sinner into a living saint. When new converts find their way to Christ, we see startling transformations since love is able to do what no man can.

Norman Vincent Peal once said, *"That love is the most curative force known to man."* It is praying with this knowledge in mind that makes prayer a truly amazing power available to everyone. In our own ministry, Rita and I have seen the impossible performed by God, as people opened themselves to the healing power of love. Yes, cancers, heart disease, Crohn's disease, blindness and even deafness have disappeared as the person was touched by God's perfect love.

Through the years when the Spirit of love has touched our meetings, all kinds of conversions have taken place. Alleged notorious sinners have come to Christ and have been transformed by His love. We could literally see ugliness leave their faces as the Holy Spirit gave them the gift of eternal life. These precious souls were not only touched by His love, but also given a whole new meaning to their lives. God's love is capable of doing anything.

People in the Church today do not pray for the necessary explosion of God's love upon them. A real renewal and revival will not break out in our nation until the saints have prayed down the love of God. The love of God can change any situation, regardless of how hopeless it might appear. As we unconsciously breathe every day, our souls should also be breathing prayer. Prayer is allowing the deep inward movement of God's Holy Spirit to do in us what He longs to do. We might say that this is the greatest of all graces in allowing God free access to our inner being. It truly can become heaven on earth.

To experience God's personal love in prayer should never be a rare event. It should be something that we expect on a daily basis. Do you have a fixed time to pray each day? Not that prayer should be routine, but prayer should be included in each and every aspect of our daily living. This helps keep our minds focused on the Eternal, which is never felt as an obligation but always as a delight. It is in this humble manner that we daily learn of God's love and concern for each of us.

As we awaken from a good night's sleep, it then becomes imperative to renew our desire for prayer and His love. Of course, each day will be different, but His unseen presence should be enjoyed the entire day. Let the love of Christ guide your every moment of every day. As your life becomes a colloquy with God, let His love be the force to draw others to Him. People will know you are different without ever having to tell them of your inward disposition toward Christ. Your prayer life and God's love in you will be more than obvious. You will radiate the glory of God unconsciously, and people will eventually realize that you have spent time in the presence of the Eternal.

Things to consider:

His great love for me can be found in prayer. Love is the most powerful healing force known to mankind. God's love for me will never change. Prayer is that surety that this love can be renewed on a daily basis. Great change of character becomes possible as prayer allows me to bask in His loving presence. As my soul moves in the direction of the Holy, my life will become filled with His loving Person. Ministry will no longer be a chore but an enjoyable delight.

Pray something like this:

Heavenly Father, thank You that You love me so very much. Please give me the grace to let this love not only transform me but others who are around me. Let me realize that it is not necessarily in speaking about You but letting others see You in me that will bring about the salvation of countless people. In Christ's name I pray. Amen.

What is Prayer?

<u>My verse for today is</u>:
"I exhort therefore, that, first of all, supplications, prayers, intercessions, and giving of thanks, be made for all men" *(1 Timothy 2:1)*.

In the early Church, prayer was considered a means of simply having a loving conversation between the soul and God, as between a child and his/her father. This is easy to understand, but it is somewhat limited on our part.

E. W. Kenyon, in his book <u>In His Presence</u>, says, "Prayer is our need crying out for help. Prayer is the voice of Faith to the Father. Prayer is born then of the sense of need, and the assurance that the need will be met."[1] [15]

Some of the monks during the Middle Ages considered prayer as being "the soul breathing."[2] [16] It was thought since we have to breathe continuously, so we must pray continuously. These are all good thoughts. But how does prayer relate to my present life? Do I need to pray as often as possible during the course of the day? These are most interesting questions that can only be answered by you. Do you really want to know God?

The first step in answering the question is to comprehend that prayer is multi-layered. First, prayer is worship, and worship is enacted in various ways. There are elements of worship, adoration, thanksgiving, confession, petition and intercession, which will eventually find their place in sincere prayer. Again, only you can decide how far you will go into the realm of the Spirit and of prayer.

The disciples of Jesus asked Him, **"Lord, teach us to pray."** Jesus said to them; **"When ye pray, say, Our Father…"** (Luke 11:2). Here Jesus gives us an insight into powerful prayer. Prayer always begins with God. In our Lord's Prayer or the "Disciples' Prayer," it starts with the needs of others and not our personal needs. The interest and concern of God comes first in this brilliant prayer. God must be first in our prayers, or our prayers will not have the power necessary for a divine answer. As we first begin with God, our thoughts of love will be coupled with the element of faith.

Worship is our first element of prayer. Again, worship means, "to bow down or prostrate oneself."[3] [17] It is the recognition or contemplation of God as seen in the person of Jesus Christ. When we say the words, "hallowed be Thy name," it is then that we are taken into the realm of worship.

In the Old Anglican Prayer Book, the word "worship" implies worthiness on the part of the one who received the honor. This is graphically shown in Revelation 5:12; **"Worthy is the Lamb that was slain to receive…honour and glory, and blessing."** Worship is the loving application of praise to God for the Being that He is. Our spirits are taken into humility and deep reverence for the goodness of our God.

Another aspect of worship is that it can actually be wordless. [4] [18] We see this expressed in Psalm 62:5; **"My soul, wait thou only upon God; for my expectation is from him."** There are times in prayer when words become a brusque intrusion. Only silence will satisfy the soul during that time.

Thanksgiving is another aspect of prayer. Psalm 118:1 says, *"Give thanks unto the Lord."* Thanksgiving in prayer is that sincere application of God's benefits toward you and others. Thanksgiving must be considered an essential and integral part of prayer. The Scriptures encourage us to thank God constantly for His love and favor toward each of us. *"Bless the Lord, O my soul, and forget not all his benefits"* (Psalm 103:2). Again in Psalm 118:1, *"Give thanks unto the Lord; for he is good: because his mercy endureth for ever."* The Bible is filled with numerous passages thanking God for His loving-kindness that He shows to all of us.

There are so many blessings that we take for granted which ones come directly from God. Before my mother died of lung cancer, she was heard thanking God for the ability to breath freely for about ten minutes without pain. She never smoked a day in her life. She thanked God for the things we usually take for granted.

Another important element of prayer is confession.[5][19] David says in Psalm 32:5, *"I will confess my transgressions unto the Lord."* There are countless times when we forget who we are. We are children of the Most High God, but at times we stoop down and touch the filth in the world by sinning willfully. This is a form of ingratitude. Even William Shakespeare recognized the sin of ingratitude and said, "Ingratitude, thou marble-hearted friend."

There are times when we fall short of the "mark of the high calling of God." We purposefully sin. In Greek, the word confession means, "to say the same thing, to admit or declare oneself guilty of what one is accused of." When we confess our sins to God, we are agreeing with Him for our need of real repentance. We begin to see things from His perspective. We missed the mark. It is imperative that we confess our sins daily, so we may stay in fellowship with our Heavenly Father at all times For our confession to be acceptable to God, it must not be general but very specific for the sins we have committed.

There is a definite place for general confession during our prayer time since we will often forget our sins. At the same time, there comes a real need to repent of specific sins that we have committed. The moment we are aware of sin in our lives, this is the moment the sin should be confessed. If this is done sincerely, in this moment God will freely forgive us, and our loving communion with Him will be restored.

Also, there are numerous kinds of confessions mentioned in the Bible, but this chapter is not for that purpose. It would be a good thing to take time and seek out the various kinds of confessions that are necessary and available to all of us. ***"I exhort therefore, that, first of all, supplications, prayers, intercessions, and giving of thanks, be made for all men"*** (1 Timothy 2:1).

Our next area on how to pray to God is that of petition.[6][20] We might say this is turning to the man-ward aspect of prayer. Petition is that form of prayer when we seek our own needs, while intercession seeks the needs of others above our own. Petition comes from a Greek word meaning "to beg, to lack." It is used to express the needs of an individual and can refer to both man and God. The idea is that of a beggar sitting on the roadside begging for the help of the king as he goes by. It shows the destitution of the beggar and his inability to meet his own need. It conveys a cry for help.

As we approach the throne of grace with our petitions, we come humbly, believing that we will be heard and answers will come. Hebrews 4:16 gives us an idea of what petition actually is; ***"Let us therefore come boldly unto the throne of grace, that we may obtain mercy and find grace to help in the time of need."*** So we might say that petitions are both requests and pleas for needs to be met. Usually there is a specific situation or circumstance in view.

On the subject of intercession, it is quite different from petitions. In intercession, we are concerned with the needs and interests of others more than our own. It is said that intercession is the most unselfish of all prayer. The Greek word gives us the idea "to fall in with a person, to draw near so as to converse freely, and hence to have freedom of access."[7] [21] It is the idea of an ordinary person approaching the King's throne with the needs of another.

It is interesting to note that the believer acts as an intermediary between God and man. The prayer warrior forgets himself and identifies with the person he or she is praying for. The greatest example of this kind of praying is found in Genesis 18:23-33 as Abraham prays to God about the people of Sodom. Abraham has great persuasive power with God.

Things to consider:

Prayer has many aspects such as worship, thanksgiving, confession, petition and intercession. It behooves me to know and understand the various forms of prayer. By knowing how to use each, I will see great and wonderful results. As I seek God in all these aspects of prayer, it will help me in forming a "Prayer Inspired Life."

Pray something like this:

Dear Heavenly Father, I want to know how to pray effectively. Teach me how to do this in my own life. Please give me the grace and strength to learn the art of prayer so that I might be very effective in Your Kingdom. Send me the grace needed to pray for others. I ask this in Christ's name. Amen.

Sovereign Intervention

My verse for today is:
"Trust in the Lord with all thine heart; and lean not unto thine own understanding. In all thy ways acknowledge him, and he shall direct thy paths" *(Proverbs 3:5-6)*

    The idea that God can intervene in the affairs of modern man seems remote to multitudes of people. At the same time, the Bible assures us that if we pray according to His will, He will answer us. Sovereign intervention depends upon knowing the will, purpose and plan of God for our lives. These cannot be considered anything less than perfect. Sovereignty in relationship to our Lord always implies the absolute best for His children. Paul says it is also "good and acceptable." Not every believer will be ready to accept this.

    There are numerous problems that Christians experience today because we tend to interpret everything in terms of "creature comforts." We are willing to accept sovereign acts of God if pain or sorrow are not involved. There are times when everything may not be going our way. Paul had insight into this matter when he stated in Romans 8:28-29, **"And we know that God causes all things to work together for good to those who love God, to those who are called according to His purpose. For whom He foreknew, He also predestined to be conformed to the image of his Son, that he might be the firstborn among many brethren."** This Scripture teaches us that Christ-likeness is not necessarily birthed without some discomfort, or even some pain. Most likely you will see adverse circumstances in your life as you are seeking to do the sovereign will of God. Remember, when you ask anything according to His will, you might see some difficulties in the future.

Oftentimes prayer is not answered if our highest desires do not correspond with God's will. We must learn that unanswered prayer may be a gracious act of love on God's part. This is one lesson in our prayer lives that we need to learn early on.

The Prayer Inspired Life desires what God wants for us. We get some idea of this in Proverbs 3:5-6, **"Trust in the Lord with all thine heart; and lean not unto thine own understanding. In all thy ways acknowledge him, and he shall direct thy paths."** It begins with trust, but not a half-hearted trust in God. It is a trust of full surrender that permits us to see His sovereign acts. It is denying our own understanding of all things, since our understanding does not even begin to compare with God's. It is a continuous acknowledgment of Him every day of our lives. As we move to this spiritual maturity, we unconsciously accept with joy the requirements of Proverbs 3. Our prayer lives take on a new tenor of unselfish delight for the needs of others more so than our own.

As we continue in prayer, seeking the will of God, His sovereignty will become most apparent. The various shortcomings you may have will soon become less of a problem to you. Your wanting the will of God in your life will slowly bring a death stroke to all your ambitions and desires. After a period of time, it will become obvious to others that you have changed.

Prayer is God's vehicle of bringing our desires and ambitions into alignment with His will. Of course, there is a personal struggle since the old flesh will rear-up at different times. By the grace of the Holy Spirit, change will occur in your life, and it will positively affect all those you encounter.

When you are seeking a sovereign intervention in your life or the lives of others, God will not indiscriminately grant everything you request. He will grant the unselfish prayer that will bring change and enlightenment into your situation. Remember, if your desire is not in accordance with His will, He will make it very clear.

During World War II, the British people prayed earnestly for the success of their troops. At the same time, the Germans were praying for the same thing for their troops. God did not grant both sides the same request. His sovereign intervention happened to fall on the side of the British during this particular time. During the evacuation of Dun Kirk in France, the British provided their forces with hundreds of little boats to get their troops out of harm's way. The British saved nearly 100,000 men in their army since a fog kept them from being seen by the German planes that would have killed all of them. Why was His sovereign intervention on the side of the British? Perhaps the reason for this is that all of Western Civilization was saved, especially the Church of Jesus Christ.

The supreme sovereign intervention can be seen in the will of Jesus Christ in Gethsemane's Garden. Jesus Christ was the most submissive man who has ever lived. Yet, the one thing that shocked Him beyond belief was His vision of His personal destruction. He saw in the Spirit, His manner of death, and it was His comprehension that all the sin of mankind would soon be on His body; ***"Father, if thou be willing, remove this cup from me: nevertheless not my will, but thine, be done"*** (Luke 22:42). Jesus prayed to know indiscriminately the will of His Father. After perceiving what it was, He voluntarily accepted it without further question.

It is quite obvious Jesus Christ led a Prayer Inspired Life that was to benefit mankind for all time. He prayed Himself into the perfect will of God every single day of His life. There is no greater expression of love for mankind than Christ's death on the cross. His entire life was Inspired by prayer for the ultimate purpose of salvation for all of mankind.

If we are to see acts of God's sovereign intervention, we must begin to have a Prayer Inspired Life. Our lives must be filled with prayer, as we seek to know Him and be led into His perfect will. Remember the lesson we can learn from Christ in Gethsemane. Prayer is not necessarily answered just because it's not answered as we want it to be. Hebrews 5:7 (New American Standard Bible) tells us, *"In the days of His flesh, He offered up both prayers and supplications with loud crying and tears to the One able to save Him from death, and He was heard because of His piety."*

All of Christ's prayers were answered, but not according to His human cravings. During His life, Jesus Christ never sinned, and His life had the fragrance of the sweet aroma of the Holy Spirit. He prayed constantly for the will of His Father to be done. It is such a life that is Prayer Inspired.

Things to consider:

Sovereign interventions we all desire to see can only be brought about through prayer. Prayer must become my life's one main object. If change in my life for the better is desired, daily prayer is most important. The force of prayer is obtainable within life if it is sought after unselfishly. The only force holding this back from manifestation is the lack of faith and diligent prayer.

Pray something like this:

Heavenly Father, You are the God of all things, and I know You do grant sovereign interventions. May my prayer life be so effective that as I pray for others, divine sovereign interventions will be manifested for Your glory. May my life begin to show that it is inspired by prayer. In Christ's name. Amen.

Delayed Prayer

<u>My verse for today is</u>:
"And when ye stand praying, forgive, if ye have ought against any: that your Father also which is in heaven may forgive you your trespasses" (Mark 11:25).

"The principal cause of my leanness and unfruitfulness is due to an unaccountable backwardness to pray. I can write or read or converse or hear with a ready heart; but prayer is more spiritual and inward than any of these, and the more spiritual any duty is the more my carnal heart is apt to start from it. I have long since learned that, if ever I was to be a minister, faith and prayer must make me one. When I can find my heart in frame and liberty by prayer, everything else is comparatively easy." (Richard Newton)

We live in an age and time where we have become accustomed to instant gratification. We have instant coffee, instant rice, instant potatoes, instant grits and the list seems to be endless. We are not used to waiting for things in this life, but sometimes in prayer, we will have to wait for an answer. There are various reasons why prayers are delayed, and we never like to know that God will make us wait. I believe that God, at times, will allow us to wait before our answer comes to fruition.

God is absolute love, but still He keeps His children waiting for prayer answers. God is love, and He seeks our love as we pray. I believe that if love does not know how to wait on God, then perhaps it is not really love on our part. God is always in the process of giving Himself to us. His heart's desire is that we learn how to give love to Him as well as others. God gave Himself to us through His Son Jesus Christ and now seeks that we give ourselves in return to Him. In other words, until we learn the art of surrendering ourselves to Him, we might be waiting on Him for an awfully long time.

We know in the natural world that love is based on esteem. How good a person looks, their style of clothing and even the car they drive, all influence us. This is all so superficial! We love only those things that we value. This has very little to do with our walk in the Spirit. That which seems to come to us so easily is not truly valued or appreciated.

We know that in the universe the laws govern the rotation of planets and stars. We neither know all the laws nor can we define them in terms readily grasped. We know that real treasures are always hard to find, but once obtained, they are esteemed beyond measure. It is a similar principle in the prayer life of an individual who acquisitions prayer answers; it's a call for proportionate efforts. God could keep us waiting until we come into that place where we are willing and motivated to keep praying for the answer's manifestation.

The first thing we need to understand in delayed answers to prayers is that God Himself is the treasure that we should be seeking. Sometimes we do not do this, and prayer seems to be stalled. If He would easily answer all our prayers, then we might just begin to take Him for granted. This is a real problem in the 21st Century. We take things for granted and want it here and now or else. This is the wrong type of heart to have in going to the Father.

Prayer is a continual activity that, after a time, comes into a deeper development and greater satisfaction on the part of the praying person. It becomes a source of both spiritual and personal satisfaction and determines our spiritual direction. God will impose time limits on prayer not for His satisfaction, but for our spiritual growth and progress. Remember that God sees things far ahead of what we are capable of seeing. The prayer that persists, in spite of a supposed no answer from God, may be a true test of spiritual persistence. Your answer will come, but perhaps not in the way you thought it would.

There are other reasons why a force as powerful as prayer may not be answered. Let us not forget that there is the world, the flesh and the devil. These three can create hindrances in receiving answers to our prayers. Some people think that prayer answers should come immediately but really don't take the necessary time in praying them through. Again there are those who pray for things they truly don't need. The result of receiving these things would only satisfy selfish fleshly desires. James 4:3 says, **"Ye ask, and receive not, because ye ask amiss, that ye may consume it upon your lusts."**

Getting back to our basic assumption, our purpose in life is to glorify God Himself. 1 Corinthians 10:31 tells us **"Whether therefore ye eat, or drink, or whatsoever ye do, do all to the glory of God."** If prayer is to be effective, it must be free of selfish interests. Like John Knox of Scotland who prayed: "Give me Scotland or I die!" Selfish interests were not involved. Scotland did experience great revival, and the Presbyterian Church was formed.

Delay is not necessarily unanswered prayer. Look at the case of Lazarus who was used to give the world a most wonderful miracle. Lazarus, who was dead, came back to life at the Lord's command. John 11:11 says, **"These things said he: and after that he saith unto them, Our friend Lazarus sleepeth; but I go, that I may awake him out of sleep** (verse 25). **Jesus said unto her, I am the resurrection, and the life: he that believeth in me, though he** *were dead, yet shall he live."* After four days in the tomb, Lazarus was raised from the dead. What a profound miracle! Can you imagine for just a moment the conversation Lazarus had with Jesus? Talk about answered prayer!

There can be hindrances to prayer because of broken relationships. It is very possible that a husband's prayer may not be answered, since he has a broken relationship with his wife. The Bible says in 1 Peter 3:7, *"Likewise, ye husbands, dwell with them according to knowledge, giving honour unto the wife, as unto the weaker vessel, and as being heirs together of the grace of life; that your prayers be not hindered."*

Another great obstacle to answered prayer is "sin." Sin can be an awful barrier to answered prayer. It behooves us to seek the Holy Spirit about sin in our lives. The prophet Isaiah speaks of this in Isaiah 59:1-2, *"Behold, the Lord's hand is not shortened, that it cannot save; neither his ear heavy, that it cannot hear: But your iniquities have separated between you and your God, and your sins have hid his face from you, that he will not hear."* And King David says in Psalm 66:18, *"If I regard iniquity in my heart, the Lord will not hear me."* As children of God, we must avoid setting up idols in our hearts. In Ezekiel 14:3 it states, *"Son of man, these men have set up their idols in their heart, and put the stumbling block of their iniquity before their face: should I be enquired of at all by them?"* Our idols of today can be money, cars, food, houses, jobs, etc. All of these eventually take our eyes off Christ.

One issue I have often spoken about is the need to forgive others for their shortcomings. An unforgiving spirit will hinder answer to prayer. Mark 11:25 says, *"And when ye stand praying, forgive, if ye have ought against any: that your Father also which is in heaven may forgive you your trespasses."*

It is also imperative to consider the poor among you. We need to reach out to the less fortunate and aid them whenever possible. Proverbs 21:13 says, *"Whoso stoppeth his ears at the cry of the poor, he also shall cry himself, but shall not be heard."* Christian generosity is imperative. Many prayers are not answered if we have not been helping in aiding the unfortunate.

It is important to ask according to God's will for your life. James 4:3 says, *"Ye ask, and receive not, because ye ask amiss, that ye may consume it upon your lusts."* Above all, remember you have an arch-enemy, satan, who will do all that he can to stop answers to your prayers. The prophet Daniel is an excellent example of one who fought the devil for twenty-one days (Daniel 10:12-13) and won.

Things to consider:

It is imperative that I learn to pray according to the will of God. Momentary pleasures must never get in my way of prayer. Things must not be allowed to become idols in my heart. Forgiving others is a sure way of seeing more answers to my prayers. It is also necessary to remember the needy and poor and do whatever possible to help them. Lastly, I must renounce the devil in my life since he will do all that he can to prevent answered prayer.

Pray something like this:

Dear Heavenly Father, by the power of Your Holy Spirit, show me anything in my heart or life that is preventing answers to my prayers. Please give me the grace to live above any idols that may have found a place in my heart. Help me to take what I have and help the poor and needy. I ask this in Christ's name. Amen.

Prayer of Agreement

<u>My verse for today is</u>:
"Again I say unto you, That if two of you shall agree on earth as touching any thing that they shall ask, it shall be done for them of my Father which is in heaven" *(Matthew 18:19)*.

"*Verily I say unto you, Whatsoever ye shall bind on earth shall be bound in heaven: and whatsoever ye shall loose on earth shall be loosed in heaven. Again I say unto you, That if two of you shall agree on earth as touching any thing that they shall ask, it shall be done for them of my Father which is in heaven. For where two or three are gathered together in my name, there am I in the midst of them*" (Matthew 18:18-20). I first learned about the power of Prayer of Agreement through the late evangelist Kenneth E. Hagin. While we were living in England, I came across one of his books on prayer that explained the Prayer of Agreement. My wife, Rita, and I pray accordingly and have seen amazing results.

Many Christians have little understanding of prayer so it is not surprising they do not comprehend the power of agreement.

The Bible is full of promises concerning prayer, but so few of us take the time to know or practice them. The Biblical promises are there for us to use and benefit from.

Carefully read Matthew 18:18-20 and then let us look especially at verse 19; *"It shall be done for them of my Father which is in heaven."* There is no greater declaration of an individual when he says "I shall" or "I will." This is a most powerful statement that Jesus said in Scripture, *"It shall be done for them of my Father which is in heaven."* Again Jesus states in John 14:14 *"If ye shall ask any thing in my name, I will do it."* These are strong assertions made by our Lord that He truly meant. We are now being confronted with a power that can be released forever as we learn to pray.

As we study verse 20 of Matthew chapter 18 we read, *"For where two or three are gathered together in my name, there am I in the midst of them."* Normally we would conclude that Jesus is speaking of an official church meeting. In actuality, He was speaking of a gathering of believers who are in total agreement. He would be, by His Spirit, in the very center of the activity. He was making it clear that whatever we bind on earth shall be bound in heaven, and whatever we loose on earth would also be loosed in heaven. God has given every believer the spiritual authority to bind and to loose.

Unfortunately, many good Christians do not know how to use this authority. The result of this ignorance is that the devil binds them. At the same time, many believe they are defeated and depressed, since they don't exercise their spiritual authority. Many do not realize they don't have to take this spiritual awkwardness from the devil. Only if they would come to the knowledge of using the Prayer of Agreement, their problems would become fewer and fewer.

Rita and I were living in the South of England. We had been given a small amount of money by a dear friend to purchase property for a Bible college. We found a most appropriate estate for a college, but the price was beyond what we could afford. We prayed and fasted about this matter, and we were impressed to make an offer well below the asking price. Within three days, we owned the property. It was the power of agreement that got us the property where hundreds of young people would eventually be trained in the Word of God.

When we act in faith, and make a choice about doing something, then the answer will come. It sounds so simple and, it is that simple. Again we see in Deuteronomy 32:30, *"How should one chase a thousand, and two put ten thousand to flight, except their Rock had sold them, and the Lord had shut them up?"* In our own ministry for the past thirty years, we have witnessed what a husband and wife can do together in prayer that can be outstanding. Over and over again Rita and I have prayed for so many sick people to be healed, and many were healed. We have encountered very difficult situations that required much determined prayer, and we've seen prayer victories.
God honors His Word regardless of who the person might be.

Now let us look at Romans 8:26, *"Likewise the Spirit also helpeth our infirmities: for we know not what we should pray for as we ought: but the Spirit itself maketh intercession for us with groanings which cannot be uttered."* The best translation of the last phrase of this verse is, *"with groanings that cannot be uttered in articulate speech."* This verse does include both groanings and praying in tongues. There aren't many people who have experienced groaning in the Spirit, but once you do experience this, it is profound. Your prayers will certainly be answered.

Now Paul speaks again about praying in the Spirit in 1 Corinthians 14:14 when he says, *"For if I pray in an unknown tongue, my spirit prayeth, but my understanding is unfruitful."* The Amplified Bible translates this passage in this manner, *"My spirit, by the Holy Spirit within me, prayeth."* There are countless times during the course of a day that I do not know how to pray for someone or something. Our natural minds are not that gifted for us to know all circumstances surrounding the many prayer needs. So I pray with the help of the Spirit. Many prayers are answered since the Holy Spirit stands with me to make intercession.

You must understand this is something the Holy Spirit does with you and not apart from you. Each one of us is responsible for our own individual prayer lives. The Spirit of God "helpeth" or helps us to pray as we ought to pray. There will be things that will come out of your heart in prayer that only the Holy Spirit will know how to pray through.

Things to consider:

I must recognize that the Prayer of Agreement is a powerful form of prayer that brings answers most readily. I must find a person whom I can be in agreement with and start praying that way. I must quote Matthew 18:18-20 before I pray and then agree on issues presented to me. I must make sure that the other individual thinks the same way about the subject as I do.

Pray something like this:

Dear Heavenly Father, we come before Your throne this day. Father, my friend needs a new job as a chemist, and we agree according to Matthew 18:19 that he has his new job. Father, we agree that his salary will be more than adequate to support his family and his lifestyle. We stand together in this agreement. We ask this in the name of Jesus Christ. Amen.

Praying Continuously

<u>My verse for today is</u>:
"And that ye put on the new man, which after God is created in righteousness and true holiness" *(Ephesians 4:24)*.

The entire idea of praying continuously is not something new, but has been a part of Church history, especially during the Middle Ages. Monasteries and convents were established under Monastic law where the majority of the twenty-four hour day was dedicated to prayer. So the thought of praying continuously is not something just recently revealed to mankind.

Jesus spoke in Luke 18:1 and said, **"And he spake a parable unto them to this end, that men ought always to pray, and not to faint."** Again this thought is expressed by Paul in 1 Thessalonians 5:17, **"Pray without ceasing."** How is this possible to be in communication with God twenty-four hours a day? Again, we see a similar thought expressed by Jesus in Matthew 26:41, **"Watch and pray, that ye enter not into temptation: the spirit indeed is willing, but the flesh is weak."**

If a man is to pray continuously day after day, hour after hour, he will soon perish for the want of sleep. He will be a very strange fellow indeed. From Luke 18:1 we are able to ascertain that all people do at times face suffering. Often we will face difficult times even when we are praying desperately. It may seem that the heavens are shut up and that God isn't really hearing our prayers. The parable in Luke 18 teaches us that we can try to change human beings with utter indifference to their real need, but we cannot change God. He cares and loves His "chosen ones." We can pray confidently while we are waiting during the testing period, knowing that God will see we "get justice, and quickly." This wonderful parable teaches us that deliverance may be sooner than first anticipated. God is acting on our behalf whether we realize this or not. We must never give up. He does hear and will act.

When I was in Seminary, I was taught that every day should be filled with prayer. This could only be accomplished by the mental attitude I would take toward my numerous tasks as a minister. Perhaps this is the attitude of being able to pray continuously. So we can see that there are things that I must do every day that require my complete attention. My mental perspective must be in the realm of prayer, realizing my duty lies before me. It is imperative that, if I am a surgeon, I keep myself totally alert during the surgery.

Paul urges us to **"Pray without ceasing"** as found in 1 Thessalonians 5:17. Again this must be understood as one's attitude toward prayer. I do my morning devotions and throughout the day I pray as I have the time. Some days I will have more time than other days. I must understand that my mental attitude must be that of prayer at all times even though it may not always be possible.

Prayer must not be seen as a duty but as a joy. Jesus prayed even during the night hours when it was necessary, but He kept the balance of prayer and communication with His disciples. It was in this manner that He kept His guard up against satan and demonic powers that would have destroyed Him and His band of disciples before the appropriate time.

We must keep our guard up against satan and his demonic power. Keeping in prayer and the attitude of prayer is the only way this can be done. Our lives are so very fragile. We live surrounded by our supernatural enemies that will cause us to sin if we let down our guard.

Paul tells us in Ephesians 6:18, *"Praying always with all prayer and supplication in the Spirit, and watching thereunto with all perseverance and supplication for all saints."* He is pointing out our need to persist in prayer against the spiritual forces of evil, since they will attempt to abort the plan of God for our lives. Paul uses the word "supplication" meaning an entreating; continued strong and incessant pleadings until the prayer is answered. There are times when prayer of this nature is really needed. He is teaching us that continuous prayer is needed since the Christian's armor will be ineffectual. There  are forces of evil today that line up against believers as never before.

We need to remain in the attitude of continuous prayer, since the days we are living in require this. At any given moment, we should be ready to pray since we may hold the answer to a miracle. Various needs will come up during the course of the day that will require your immediate response in prayer.

Near the end of chapter 6 in Ephesians, it compares the Christian to a Roman soldier dressed for battle. Paul clearly shows the Christian that he, too, is well equipped to win the spiritual battles he must fight if he puts on his armor each and every day — the helmet of salvation, breastplate of righteousness, belt of truth, shoes of peace, sword of the Spirit and shield of faith. Always being ready to pray is one great advantage in our battle against satan and demonic powers. Let prayer be the first thing we do in any given situation. God will instruct us from that point on if we trust in Him.

Things to consider:

I must understand that praying continuously in the truest sense of the word is for all Christians. There will be times during the day that prayer will be offered, but at the same time, my attitude of praying continuously is still very important. Talking to God through the entire day, whenever possible, is in a sense praying continuously. On my job, in my home, at school, and even shopping are opportunities for prayer.

Pray something like this:

Dear Heavenly Father, help me to focus all of my attention on You. Help me to remain in the attitude of prayer, and let me take every opportunity whenever possible to seek You in prayer. I ask this in Christ's name. Amen.

Common Sense and Prayer

<u>My verse for today is</u>:
"For I will give you a mouth and wisdom, which all your adversaries shall not be able to gainsay nor resist" *(Luke 21:15)*.

Spiritual life is a journey that begins with taking a single step. It is a step of faith in God's ability on our behalf. It is faith wherein when you pray, God truly hears us.

Common sense reveals the need to pray for our family, friends, and those whom we know need prayer. Common sense in the world today is not quite so common. It would appear in the lives of countless people, that common sense has taken a back door in their lives. It is prayer that brings us to that place, where common sense is once again appreciated and valued. Common sense must never be taken for granted, for it is my belief that it's one of our mental faculties that can be improved with prayer.

In relationship to common sense and prayer, we must put our feelings on a back burner and let Godly reason dictate. We need to ignore our feelings and become most attentive to our faith. It is imperative that we begin to forget about ourselves and begin to focus on God. Common sense will show a need to focus spiritually on Christ and not on the things of this life.

Prayer opens the doors of common sense where we see that God does have the whole world in His arms; but our arms are the only ones that can take Him into our hearts. The more we pray, the more it seems that common sense becomes a sharpened faculty. Our mind and intellect seem to expand beyond their ordinary limits. Prayer will fine tune common sense to the extent that we begin to do things in different ways more effectively. We see and understand people more dynamically, since prayer and common sense are developing our inner sight more precisely. Even spiritual intuition is now something we know that if we listen to it more readily, many problems can be avoided. Prayer and common sense open the spiritual door for wisdom to be multiplied in our personal life.

Common sense tells me that I must make prayer a high priority in my daily life. We use common sense to arrange our day to make adequate and sufficient time for prayer. The amount of time we allow for daily prayer tells us of the importance that prayer has in our lives. To make a radical change in my daily schedule for prayer will take a strong sense of purpose and a real reliance on the Holy Spirit. Our will always plays a definite role in the final decision-making and success of it. Paul tells us in Ephesians 3:16 that we can reinforce the inner man, as he says, **"strengthened with might through his Spirit in the inner man."** The Holy Spirit can give us spiritual energy to pray and make the time for prayer.

Those who do not take the time to pray will find themselves less fortunate than those who do. Praying people are always ahead of others. Those who don't see the need of prayer, lose a lot. Rita and I have a friend who seeks the Lord about all of her business dealings and now she is worth millions of dollars. She can see things that others cannot see. Success comes to her, since she trusts common sense and prayer. Those two ingredients are the primary initiators in her life, and her business deals grow larger and larger as the years go by.

Paul tells us in Ephesians 5:16, **"Redeeming the time, because the days are evil."** There is a price for time, and sometimes the price is very high. Prayer is not a game to be played, but a gift from God to be used for His glory. Common sense says we must not waste our time. Once it's gone – it's gone. We must pray to know how to use this precious gift from God more appropriately. Why has the devil blinded so many good people with the idea that they have all the time in the world at their disposal? Once he can get us to forget common sense, he will probably win.

It is imperative we understand there will be a continual attack in our spiritual lives. Common sense leads us to prayer to best defend us during these moments of demonic attack. Common sense tells us that the devil fears prayer because it is powerful. In Seminary, I read a book about Martin Luther who said, "What the devil fears more than anything else is the saint upon his knees." Luther certainly had this right!

In prayer, we talk to God; in response, God will talk to us. Common sense tells us when God is speaking, the devil keeps silent. Common sense teaches us to keep praying to God so we can keep the devil away. Common sense is needed when dealing with satan. The Bible tells us in Jude 9, **"Yet Michael the archangel, when contending with the devil he disputed about the body of Moses, durst not bring against him a railing accusation, but said, The Lord rebuke thee."**

The disciples of Jesus were called upon to resist the devil. In James 4:7, **"Submit yourselves therefore to God. Resist the devil, and he will flee from you."** Each and every time the devil is attempting to present a trial, prayer and common sense become vitally important. Both are essential in any type of spiritual warfare.

The problem in the Church today is that we don't use our common sense often enough. Problems arise that could cause splits in the Church, but still not enough prayer is said nor is common sense used. One day I received a phone call from someone in Washington State about a problem with his associate pastor. He was ready to throw the associate pastor out of the Church since they had a difference in opinion. I told him not to do this, because it would cause division in the Church. My counsel was that he should meet with the young man and his wife in the pastor's office and provide some light refreshments. He was instructed to take the time to listen to the young couple. By the grace of God, the entire issue was cleared up without any ill feelings. It is very unfortunate that prayer and common sense are truly lacking in the Church and the world.

Prayer and common sense are vitally important when it comes to satan wanting to steal our blessings. Many times we will get a great revelation from God's Word, and we rejoice in it. Suddenly, the blessing is gone because we let satan steal it from us. In Matthew 13:19 it says, **"When any one heareth the word of the kingdom, and understandeth it not, then cometh the wicked one, and catcheth away that which was sown in his heart. This is he which received seed by the way side."** We must guard our hearts by not allowing the devil any room whatsoever. It is in this manner that we will retain our blessings, and they will never be stolen from us.

Things to consider:

I need more common sense and prayer. Today common sense is hardly used, as it should be, so I need to pray for it to be more prevalent. Things in my life will change for the better, as I acquire common sense and pray more efficiently and effectively.

Pray something like this:

Dear Heavenly Father, please give me more common sense. Let my prayer life reflect that I have been in Your presence, seeking the most needed human characteristic known as common sense. I will give You all the glory and honor, as my prayer life becomes what it should be. Please let prayer and common sense become an every day part of my life. In Christ's name. Amen.

Intercessory Prayer

My verse for today is:
"For kings, and for all that are in authority; that we may lead a quiet and peaceable life in all godliness and honesty" (1 Timothy 2:2).

"The act of praying is the very highest energy that the human mind is capable; praying, that is, with the total concentration of the faculties. The great mass of worldly men and learned men are absolutely incapable of prayer." – Coleridge

We have briefly spoken about intercessory prayer in the chapter entitled, "What is prayer?" We have learned that intercessory prayer is praying on behalf of others. I consider it to be the highest and most selfless form of prayer that a human may exercise. The problems we are facing in the 21st Century will never be resolved without much intercession on the part of the Church. It is time that we make intercession for our nation and the world.

We find in 1 Timothy 2:1-4, an approach toward intercessory prayer, *"I exhort therefore, that, first of all, supplications, prayers, intercessions, and giving of thanks, be made for all men; For kings, and for all that are in authority; that we may lead a quiet and peaceable life in all godliness and honesty. For this is good and acceptable in the sight of God our Saviour; Who will have all men to be saved, and to come unto the knowledge of the truth."*

Here we see Timothy setting things in proper order. First, we are to pray for kings and "for all that are in authority." With our chaotic society, it certainly makes tremendous sense to pray for presidents, prime ministers, kings and queens, and rulers of nations. Oftentimes we get things all messed up because we don't follow directions. Here we are told to pray for those in authority. We must not allow secondary things to predominate our prayer list.

When the conditions in prayer are ordered accordingly, we can expect positive results. When we pray for those in authority, we are less likely to criticize them. As Christians who know Christ, we should not put political parties first, but Christ's interests must be first. Some people become so politically minded that they spiritually lose sight of Christ. The purpose for praying for those in authority is so "we may lead a quiet and peaceable life in all godliness and honesty." Our Lord is most concerned about His people and will move on their behalf, even though their leaders may not be Christians.

Please note in verse 3, Timothy says, *"For this is good and acceptable in the sight of God our Savior."* We must carry out the divine plan set forth here, or we will not see what we desire. Verse 4 says, *"Who will have all men to be saved, and to come unto the knowledge of the truth."* God's ultimate purpose in this is so we will be able to spread the Gospel. If our government is not able to keep the peace in the nation, it becomes difficult to spread the Gospel of salvation. During times of upheaval and war, it is almost impossible to spread the Gospel. In Matthew 24:14 Jesus said, *"And this gospel of the kingdom shall be preached in all the world for a witness unto all nations; and then shall the end come."* The devil will do all he can to prevent this from being accomplished.

Now that we have taken into consideration for whom we are to pray, let us now take a look at the most effective way it should be done. Carefully note that Paul said, **"supplications, prayers, intercessions."** Let us consider the topic of intercession. The prayer of intercession is, of course, a prayer for others, and this passage is talking about praying, or interceding, for others. An intercessor is one who takes the place of another and will even plead another's case before the throne of God.

An excellent example of intercessory prayer is found in Genesis 18:20-33, where we see Abraham's intercession for the cities of Sodom and Gomorrah. Abraham humbled himself before the Lord, referring to himself as "but dust and ashes." The Scriptures tell us to humble ourselves, to submit ourselves to God. **"Draw nigh to God, and he will draw nigh to you"** (James 4:8). Many people seek God to make them humble. Humility is a voluntary act of our personal will. God will not make us humble.

When Israel was dedicating Solomon's temple, God promised He would do certain things. Even if they went away into sin, when they returned to God and humbled themselves, He would hear and answer them and bring restoration. **"If my people, which are called by my name, shall humble themselves, and pray, and seek my face, and turn from their wicked ways; then I will hear from heaven, and will forgive them their sin, and will heal their land"** (2 Chronicles 7:14).

There is an important principle, a real nugget of truth, in Genesis 18, when Abraham is interceding for the cities of Sodom and Gomorrah. Imagine if Abraham would have asked: "Now, Lord, if you can find five righteous men," the Lord would have said, "All right, if I find five righteous, I won't destroy the city." I am convinced that if Abraham had continued even for the sake of one, the cities would have been spared. What a tremendous statement! "I will not destroy Sodom and Gomorrah for ten's sake." Imagine God saying that He would spare that wicked place. He had already spoken about their sin, and about their sexual impurity.

We have the ability to change things through prayer. We can hold back judgment on the unsaved and give them a little more time to hear the Gospel. I believe there are many righteous men and women in America today. I believe there are people who will take their place in prayer just as Abraham did in intercession. If we do, we will change things. By the way, it doesn't take a great number of people to do this. We just need to make intercessory prayer a priority because it is the key to our future. We must make this a part of our daily lives so we can see what a difference it will make in the lives of others.

Things to consider:

Intercessory prayer is praying on behalf of others. I can help change my nation if I will intercede for my government. The most miserable of all sinners can be saved through intercession. There are no limits when it comes to intercessory prayer.

Pray something like this:

Dear Heavenly Father, please teach me the art of intercession. Help me to see the needs of others more importantly than my own. Send Your grace upon me, and let me pray for others that they might find Christ. In Christ's name. Amen.

Prayer and Fasting

My verse for today is:
"Howbeit this kind goeth not out but by prayer and fasting" (*Matthew 17:21*).

"Howbeit this kind goeth not out but by prayer and fasting" (Matthew 17:21). From this Scripture, we see that in some cases, prayer and fasting are needed to secure deliverance. There are numerous accounts of prayer and fasting in the Bible that brought marvelous results. Moses fasted forty days before he received the Law of God on Mt. Sinai. He prayed for Israel when they committed idolatry and was threatened with national extinction (Exodus 32:10; 30-35). Moses also interceded for another forty days with prayer and fasting (Exodus 34:28). When he descended from the Mount, his face shone with the glow of one who had tarried long in the presence of God.

Elijah was triumphant over the prophets of Baal at the challenge on Mt. Carmel; nevertheless, he ran for his life since Jezebel wanted to kill him. Deep in the wilderness, he sat down under a juniper tree and sincerely wished he would die. God encouraged him, and shortly afterward, he went on a divinely appointed forty day fast (1 Kings 19:1-8). Later, he went down and met Ahab and boldly pronounced judgment on him and Jezebel for the murder of Naboth and the confiscation of the vineyard. The entire house of Ahab trembled. His stern denunciation apparently brought the wicked king to his knees in at least temporary repentance (1 Kings 21:17-29).

We see in the life of Daniel, how he sought God for the interpretation of a vision pertaining to the destiny of his people who had just returned from seventy years of captivity (Daniel 9:23-10:13). Daniel's prayer was dispatched on the first day, but a satanic adversary withstood the angel's messenger who was sent to him (10:12). Daniel continued in prayer for twenty-one days, and during that time he **"ate no pleasant bread"** (10:3). Ultimately God did send reinforcements by the Archangel Michael, and the total and full answer to his petition came. Daniel still waited upon God; he was there to receive the answer when it came.

The Lord Jesus Christ fasted and was tempted by satan for forty days and nights before He began His public ministry (Luke 4:2). Afterward, **"Jesus returned in the power of the Spirit into Galilee: and there went out a fame of him through all the region round about"** (verse 14). From that point in time, Christ's ministry was typified by countless miracles. In the Acts of the Apostles, we learn that the worldwide missionary movement was born during a time when the leaders of the Church at Antioch **"ministered to the Lord and fasted"** (Acts 13:2).

In the deliverance of the child possessed by the devil as seen in Matthew 17:14-21, we are informed of some very significant facts concerning the healing of stubborn and difficult cases. The disciples had been having notable success in praying for the sick, until they encountered a situation that they were unable to overcome. A lunatic child, (mentally ill) possessed with a demon, was brought to the disciples. To their embarrassment, they were unable to cast out the evil spirit. Perhaps they may have supposed that there was some inherent reason why the child could not be healed and delivered. Their thinking was faulty. When Jesus arrived on the scene, the child was delivered. Jesus said they lacked the faith for this type of healing. Then He explained to them more fully the cause of their unbelief. **"Howbeit, this kind goeth not out but by prayer and fasting"** (Matthew 17:21). This inference is most clear that faith to cast out certain kinds of demons comes only as the result of prayer coupled with fasting.

It is most important to do your fasting in private, not that any harm is done if someone should know. From the words of Jesus, fasting is not to draw attention or gain the approval of others. It should be done without them being aware of what you are doing. This could hinder one from achieving the very purpose of the fast. Jesus said: **"Moreover when ye fast, be not, as the hypocrites, of a sad countenance: for they disfigure their faces, that they may appear unto men to fast. Verily I say unto you, They have their reward. But thou, when thou fastest, anoint thine head, and wash thy face; That thou appear not unto men to fast, but unto the Father which is in secret: and thy Father, which seeth in secret, shall reward thee openly"** (Matthew 6:16-18).

It is important to prepare our body for fasting. Doing a long fast without proper preparation could be deadly. The body has its own cycle for fasting. The best-known cycles in which the body cycles itself are in the following order of days: 1, 3, 7, 14, 21 and 40. One must build himself up before going on a long fast. The amount of poisons in the average person's liver is paramount. These poisons must be released slowly or we could become very sick and die. So fasting must begin with one day at a time, without taking on too much too soon.

Fluids should be taken every single day in large amounts. This will help flush the kidneys and relieve the smell of toxins leaving the body. Pure distilled water is best to start on short fasts. Coffee, tea, and sodas should never be taken while fasting. Fruit juices may be consumed only if they are cut in half with distilled water. This way you will prevent pancreatic shock. Too much sugar on a fast can be damaging to the whole body. Prepare yourself over a period of weeks with short fasts of no more than three days. This will help your body in preparation for a longer fast.

Never go on a fast without drinking water or some other good liquid. If you should fast beyond three days without water, you could damage the kidneys beyond repair. There may be a need to have an enema several times a week, if you are going to do a long fast. Again, caution must be used in regards to fasting. If you are a diabetic, you should not fast! You could kill yourself.

Fasting cannot replace our need of obedience to the other commands of Scripture. Samuel said to Saul, who had disobeyed the commandment of the Lord, **"Behold, to obey is better than sacrifice"** (1 Samuel 15:22). During the time of Zechariah, the people fasted indeed, but their hearts had not been prepared to serve the Lord. They did not obey His commandments, nor "**did they hearken unto the voice of the Lor**d" or "**show mercy and compassions every man to his brother**" (Zechariah 7:9). Consequently, their prayers and fastings were in vain. God did not hear them.

In fasting, one should have a set goal in mind, so God is glorified during that time. There must be a purpose for the fast, if there are to be answered prayers. In Isaiah 58:3-6 the Lord complains that some fasted for debate and strife to make their **"voice to be heard on high."** Let not the body of Christ be as foolish as they were in Isaiah's day. Our intentions and purposes for fasting must have Godly spiritual qualities. **"Then shall thy light break forth as the morning, and thine health shall spring forth speedily: and thy righteousness shall go before thee; the glory of the Lord shall be thy reward"** (Isaiah 58:8).

I am often asked the question, when should I fast? It is important that we follow a Scriptural course. There should be a real reason for fasting. Again, we should have a definite object in view. It would be tremendous if churches would unite and have certain days each month to fast for the protection of the United States. Nineveh listened to God's message and truly repented. ***"So the people of Nineveh believed God, and proclaimed a fast, and put on sackcloth, from the greatest of them even to the least of them"*** (Jonah 3:5). And God graciously ***"saw their works"*** and spared that city of about 120,000 souls.

Is there not such a great crisis upon us even today? Greater than the crisis of Nineveh, is the crisis upon this country and the world. The day of the Lord is surely approaching. "Who shall be able to stand?" Indeed, it is time for the entire Church to be called to mourning and fasting, lest they be accounted as those of the Laodicean Church, who were neither hot or cold, but had to be removed from the Lord's mouth (Revelations 3:14-19).

Some people are waiting for a convenient time when the Lord will put a fast upon them. This is not going to happen. Remember, fasting is not a pleasure, but self-denial. I have met many Christians who have told me that they have fasted ten, twenty, thirty and forty days to see no results of their fasting. Again fasting must be accompanied with much prayer and faith.

Therefore, in the Prayer Inspired Life, fasting may be a spiritual force used for good. Mountains can be moved if fasting is coupled with faith and prayer. The Prayer Inspired Life is not an ordinary life, since we are dealing with spiritual powers and forces that we can control by prayer and fasting.

Things to consider:

I must understand that fasting is not optional, but required in my life if I am to be spiritually successful. The Prayer Inspired Life is afforded power over spiritual forces, which do respond to prayer and fasting. I must use common sense when fasting and always drink pure water during that time. I must never fast without water, because I could possibly do great damage to my kidneys and body. If I am going on an extended fast, I must be sure to build myself up to this spiritual adventure. Lastly, I must remember that fasting requires both prayer and faith.

Pray something like this:

Dear Heavenly Father, grant me the grace and wisdom to fast. Show me what I should fast for each new time I exercise this holy sacrifice. Teach me the secret of prayer coupled with faith during my fast. I will give You all the praise and the glory. In Christ's name. Amen.

Claiming Your Promises

<u>My verse for today is</u>:
"Not that I speak in respect of want: for I have learned, in whatsoever state I am, therewith to be content" *(Philippians 4:11)*.

"Whereby are given unto us exceeding great and precious promises: that by these ye might be partakers of the divine nature, having escaped the corruption that is in the world through lust" (2 Peter 1:4).

The Bible is full of great and precious promises made by God to humankind. There are literally thousands of promises that God has made, offering a completely new glorious lifestyle for those who seek them. The great English Evangelist Charles Haddon Spurgeon once said, "Every promise of Scripture is a writing of God, which may be pleaded before Him with this reasonable request. 'Do as Thou hast said'. The Creator will not cheat the creature that depends upon His truth; and far more, the Heavenly Father will not break His word to His own child."[1] [22]

A Scriptural promise is a written or verbal declaration that binds the individual who makes it, to act accordingly. When used of God, it becomes His pledge to act or refrain from doing certain things. It is said such promises are the basis of prayer coupled with faith. In other words, if God has said something especially to you, He will do it. It is through our prayer that these promises are turned into the reality of our Christian experience.

The validity of the promises is dependent upon the character of the One who has made them. God has made thousands of promises to His children. However, they will never see the manifestation of these promises, unless they have faith to believe in them. The author of Hebrews says, **"Let us hold fast the profession of our faith without wavering; for he is faithful that promised"** (Hebrews 10:23). God is a God who does not lie. His infinite power makes all things possible. Any promise He has made can come to pass if the individual will move in faith.

As we come to God with one of His promises, we can be like Abraham who had unwavering trust. **"He staggered not at the promise of God through unbelief; but was strong in faith, giving glory to God; And being fully persuaded that, what he had promised, he was able also to perform"** (Romans 4:20-21). Let us not forget that Abraham and Sarah were promised a son who would be born to them in their old age. Abraham was one hundred years of age, and Sarah was ninety. Yet, God said it would happen, and it did. Why did they have to wait so long for a son? Their faith level was never high enough to receive their son. It goes back to us believing God's Word.

Therefore, we come to that special place in prayer where we have to confess what the Word of God says about our situation. If we continually make a confession of failure, sickness, or lack thereof, we will not receive the promise. Our faith or unbelief will be declared by what we say or confess. Very few people have the right understanding of how the spoken word can affect our hearts and our adversary. In all this, our prayer lives and successes are dependent on our confession. We cannot rise above our confession, so it is important to change our confession. We need to start saying and praying what God has to say about every situation. By confessing God's Word, we will begin to move out of the sense realm into a new spiritual realm.

Hebrews 4:14 must become our daily companion on this spiritual journey: *"Having then a great high priest, who hath passed through the heavens, Jesus the Son of God, let us hold fast our confession."* Our confession should be that the Word of God is true, and we should speak this over the promise God has given us. When we doubt God's Word, we doubt Him. Doubt will incapacitate prayer. Faith filled prayers, with the promises of God, will come to pass. If there is anything in our lives that seems to contradict the Word of God, it will destroy the power of our prayer. This in turn could bring us into great spiritual bondage.[2] [23]

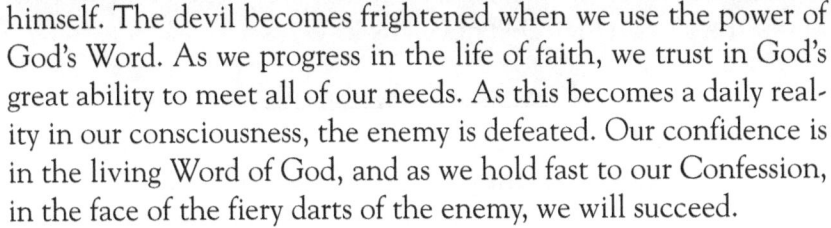

In the Prayer Inspired Life, if we are going to live and walk by faith, we will be tested. The testing does not come from God but from the enemy (devil) himself. The devil becomes frightened when we use the power of God's Word. As we progress in the life of faith, we trust in God's great ability to meet all of our needs. As this becomes a daily reality in our consciousness, the enemy is defeated. Our confidence is in the living Word of God, and as we hold fast to our Confession, in the face of the fiery darts of the enemy, we will succeed.

I love how Dr. Moffat translates 2 Corinthians 2:14-15: *"Wherever I go, I thank God, He makes my life a constant pageant of triumph in Christ, diffusing the perfume of his knowledge everywhere by me. I live for God as the fragrance of Christ breathed alike by those who are being saved and by those who are perishing."*[3] [24] As we speak over our prayers what God's Word has to say about them, the reality of His precious and great promises will manifest. As we walk in the light of Christ, we begin to realize that our faith will never go beyond our confession.

Claiming Your Promises

The Word of God becomes real only as we stand on it daily. This means we have to confess it in our prayers. ***"For we walk by faith, not by sight"*** (2 Corinthians 5:7). As a doctor, I have been trained in the sense realm of knowledge when dealing with patients. There is another realm of knowledge that includes the Spirit and God's Word, which supersedes sense realm knowledge. When we confess what God has to say about any subject, satan is frightened.

The Prayer Inspired Life is a life of continual victory. Remember, there is no need greater than Christ's ability to meet that need. Confess what God's Word has to say about your prayers, and the answers will come.

Things to consider:

I realize there are thousands of promises in God's Word, and they are mine when I claim them. When I pray over these promises and claim them, I must say what God's Word says about them. My prayer life depends upon my faith in the integrity of God to do what He has said in His Word. By faith, all things are possible, if I will get out of the way and let God have His way.

Pray something like this:

Dear Heavenly Father, I come to You in Jesus Christ's name. I want to know and understand the power of Your exceedingly great promises. Help me to speak Your Word over all the promises that I claim by faith. Help me to let my life show others that I am being Inspired by Prayer. In Christ's name. Amen.

Watch Your Mouth

My verse for today is:
"**Thou art snared with the words of thy mouth, thou art taken (captive) with the words of thy mouth**" (*Proverbs* 6:2).

It is important in the realm of the Spirit that we learn to speak positively. We cannot afford the luxury of negative thinking or negative speaking. Life and death, at times, may be determined by what we do say or don't say. When we think we can't do something and confess this negatively, we will never be able to accomplish it. When dealing with terminal illness, it is absolutely imperative that no negative words are spoken when claiming healing.

Negative people and negative talk must not be around when we need a miracle. Even people in the world know this principle. Words have the ability to heal or cause demise. Proverbs 6:2 says: *"**Thou art snared with the words of thy mouth, thou art taken (captive) with the words of thy mouth.**"* It cannot get any clearer than this: We must be utterly cautious as to what we say when seeking God for a miracle.

The words coming from our mouth can mean liberation or domination. What we say about ourselves must be according to God's Word. This will bring a new confidence that will take possession of us. This then will encourage our faith, as we are on our way to healing or even a miracle.

We must remember that God's ability is working on our behalf when we speak the Word positively. We are being healed every moment of the day! Our miracle is in our mouth. Words are more powerful than any tank or bomb. They will work on our behalf if we use them correctly. The words we speak can either become a task-master or a servant working on our behalf. It is totally dependent on our ability to begin to speak positively about our healing, marriage, finances, job, etc. It is up to us to change our circumstances, or things will not change.

Our mouth has the ability to make us a millionaire or a pauper! When our words are filled with faith, we will be amazed at how people want to be around us. When we project love through what we speak, we have the ability to melt the heart of the most hardened of all sinners. Our blessings or curses are in the power of what we speak.

Oftentimes it is very difficult to control what we think. It is far more difficult to control what we speak. *We don't have to talk negatively about anyone or anything.* Our faith is totally dependent on what we say. What we say can change the most difficult of circumstances totally around for the good. Our language can be filled with hate speech or love speech. Things will be totally different when we begin to speak the language of love.

Now the master of hate speech was none other than Adolph Hitler. By his hate speech, he was able to turn an entire nation against the Jewish race. As a result of his occult speech, over six million Jews lost their lives in the concentration death camps. Jesus spoke in such a manner that people would respond positively to

His words. People were healed, delivered from demonic oppression, raised from the dead, and thousands of people were fed. This was done by the power of Jesus' positive speech. He spoke the Word of God, and glorious things took place.

The words of Jesus Christ cause faith to grow in our hearts. Our own speech should become more like His, since it will cause others to want what we have. Healing and health are in our mouths far more than we realize.

We need to think in a new dimension. We need to cultivate this habit of thinking, so our speech will cause our spirits to become totally victorious. This whole new way of thinking and speaking will revolutionize our prayer lives. We will pray more boldly with greater results as we exercise our faith. We will begin to see that what we confess with our mouths will become a reality in the natural realm.

The Prayer Inspired Life will feed faith to those around us. They will see that we operate on a whole new spiritual dimension, and our speech reflects this profound new aspect of our being. The spiritual diversionary tactics used by satan will no longer be used successfully to guide us into defeat. His charted tactics will become known before they happen. We will recognize the Holy Spirit telling us within our spirit, that it's time to pray. Our prayer life will then reflect this internal adjustment to victory.

The Prayer Inspired Life is a life of humility, always realizing that it is God who is guiding us into new areas of success. Everything brought to the Father in prayer is brought to Him in faith. Life becomes worth living each new day, because it will be filled with peace, power and purpose. Our lives will be controlled by love, and no longer can any negativity have a place in our speech. This is the power of prayer when one enters into the Prayer Inspired Life. Life becomes full of Christ and answers to prayers come, as we wait upon the Lord.

Things to consider:

What I say or don't say can determine my future. If I am seeking a healing or a miracle from God, the power often lies in my mouth. Negative words bring negative events and unfulfilled prayer. The Prayer Inspired Life brings peace, power and purpose to my existence.

Pray something like this:

Dear Heavenly Father, please help me to speak positively about everything that may come into my life. Help me learn to say those things that You would say about any given person, event or situation. May my speech reflect the indwelling Christ. In Christ's name. Amen.

Battle of the Mind

My verse for today is:
"Sanctify them through thy truth: thy word is truth" (*John 17:17*).

It is necessary as we begin this chapter to understand that we have an enemy who will not stop oppressing the saints of God. Satan and his demon power can "oppress" a child of God by tormenting the mind, the will and the emotions. Satan cannot possess a Christian, but he can possess a non-Christian. Demons can cause havoc with a non-Christian, but not with a Christian who knows who he is in Christ.

The devil hates believers since he cannot possess them and make them become his slaves. He will do anything to kill us, but it will not happen, since God has a supernatural hedge of protection around us. A body that is not totally controlled by demon power will never kill itself. On the contrary, a body given to satan and demon power is a target for suicide. Today we see this among many young people, especially in America and Western Europe.

Demon spirits do hinder the spread of the Gospel. In Matthew 13:19 it says, *"The wicked shall catch away the seed that was sown in the heart."* This is one of Christ's great teaching parables that implies what is sown in the heart can be caught away. When God's Word is spoken, it will enter our heart, and we will believe it. Confusion often comes, and soon the Word that was sown in us, slowly departs if symptoms of an illness reappear. This is one of satan's countless ways of deceiving Christians and robbing them of God's blessings.

Perhaps you walked in spiritual victory for weeks in an area of your Christian walk that you thought you had the victory over. Unfortunately, the seed was not watered with prayer and God's Word, and your problem returned. The devil managed to steal that which was sown in your heart. When the devil begins to bombard our mind, will and emotions, the seed that was sown does not have enough time to germinate or grow.

When Rita and I did missionary work in Haiti, we actually saw humble farmers plant their corn seeds and then dig them up again in a few days. They ate their seed and did not produce a harvest. This is a similar principle that we find among Christians who had the seed sown in their hearts only to find later that it was dug up a few days later. We must protect that which has been given to us by the Precious Word of God.

One of satan's chief goals is to get Christians to doubt the Word of God. He said to Eve in Genesis 3:4, *"Ye shall not surely die. God said you would die, but you will not surely die."* God's Word tell us, "*I can do all things through Christ which strengthens me"* (Philippians 4:13). And the devil comes along and says, "Yes, it says that, but do you really think it means that?" All kinds of doubt is sent against the Christian's mind to keep him in turmoil and doubt. Isaiah 53:4 says, *"Surely he hath borne our griefs, and carried our sorrows"* and that is exactly what was meant. The enemy comes along once again to bring confusion and doubt as to if we really can be healed. The mind becomes bombarded with all kinds of doubts concerning God's ability on our behalf.

Things to consider:

My mind can become a battlefield of torment and doubt if I let it. Satan wishes to steal God's Word from my heart and keep me in spiritual infancy, never experiencing true Christian maturity. I must guard my heart at all times from doubt and unbelief. God, by the power of prayer, will deliver me from all satanic schemes. Prayer is the means by which satan and demon powers become defeated. The Word of God must continuously be in my heart so I can grow and take gigantic steps of faith in the Kingdom of God.

Pray something like this:

Dear Heavenly Father, I ask You to give me the grace and strength to protect my heart and mind from all satanic oppression. Help me to become full of faith. Let my life reflect the presence of Your Holy Spirit to others. I ask You to increase my desire for Your Word in my life. In Christ's name. Amen.

The Prayer of Commitment

<u>My verse for today is</u>:

"**And we know that all things work together for good to them that love God, to them who are the called according to his purpose**" *(Romans 8:28)*.

There are times in our prayer lives when we pray about problems or situations with seemingly very little results. Often this is the result of not praying according to the will of God.

Many years ago, while living in Manchester, England I came across a book which talked about the Prayer of Commitment. The Apostle Peter spoke about this kind of prayer when he said, **"Casting all your care upon him; for he careth for you"** (1 Peter 5:7). The Amplified Bible expands this verse into some detail. It says, **"Casting the whole of you - all your anxiety, all your worries, all your concern, once and for all - on Him; for He cares for you affectionately, and cares about you watchfully."** This certainly does bring more light to this verse. It is a most liberating experience to be able to lay all our cares on Jesus Christ.

While we learn to pray the Prayer of Commitment, we must not forget about the laws governing prayer. If we will take the time to learn about the Prayer of Commitment, it will help eliminate some of the things we are praying about. Some Christian prayers are not being answered because they are not doing what God said to do about cares, anxieties, worries and concerns. They are not doing what they should be doing, since they haven't been properly taught what to do.

Everything we do in prayer must be in accordance with the Bible. We need to know what God's Word has to say about our prayer intention. This is the Prayer of Commitment, the prayer of laying all our cares and burdens upon Him. God's Word says, **"Commit thy way unto the Lord; trust also in him; and he shall bring it to pass"** (Psalm 37:5). He is not going to do it for us. This is something that each one of us must do. He cannot take it away until we do it exactly. God desires not only to lighten our load or burden, but to take it all. We must realize that we must play a vital role in the Prayer of Commitment.

It is not God's desire that His children worry or fret, to be filled with anxiety or burdened with the cares of this life. There is something required of all of us. In an imperative sentence, such as those in 1 Peter 5:7 and Psalm 37:5, the subject of the sentence is understood to be "you." The Lord said, **"Casting all your care upon him…"** (You) commit your way unto the Lord. We must do our part, by releasing our problems to Him, before He can take over our situation.

When we truly cast our burdens and cares upon God and commit our way unto Him, they are no longer ours but the Lord's. They are gone from us. They are no longer in our hands, but in His. There is so much the Lord would have done for us, but we hold onto things which prevent Him from doing them. We may have been most sincere and honest in our prayers, but never saw any real results. This could be the result of not praying according to His Word. We wonder why things don't work out for us; we prayed, but not according to the dictates of the Word. It behooves us to come to know the Word of God.

There are times when we pray that God will lift the cares and burdens from us. There may be other times when this happens, that we go back to the altar and take our cares and burdens back out of His hands. You cannot get the victory in this situation if you keep doing this.

We read in Matthew 6:25-27 the following; *"Therefore I say unto you, Take no thought for your life, what ye shall eat, or what ye shall drink; nor yet for your body, what ye shall put on. Is not the life more than meat, and the body more than raiment? Behold the fowls of the air: for they sow not, neither do they reap, nor gather into barns; yet your heavenly Father feedeth them. Are ye not much better than they?"* Jesus was saying, *"Which of you by working and being overly anxious is going to change anything?"*

Worry is a constant agitation that doesn't get you very far in this life. Luke's Gospel records the same passage and he says, *"And he said unto his disciples, Therefore, I say unto you, Take no thought for your life, what ye shall eat; neither for the body, what ye shall put on" (Luke 12:22).* Another similar translation of this verse reads, *"Be not anxious about tomorrow."*

Naturally, we have to plan and prepare for tomorrow; it is essential that we make certain provisions for the future. But the Lord is teaching us that He doesn't want us to be filled with anxiety and worry about tomorrow. Jesus Christ will see us through all our tomorrows as we learn to let Him lead us into what He has for us. It becomes a matter of trust for those who will enter the Prayer Inspired Life.

Worry has the power to nullify our prayers. Paul says in Philippians 4:6; *"Be careful for nothing; but in every thing by prayer and supplication with thanksgiving let your requests be made known unto God."* The Amplified translation of this verse can assist us as it says, **"Do not fret or have any anxiety about anything."** Again "you" is to be the understood subject of the sentence. When the Lord said, **"Be careful (anxious) for nothing"** He is literally saying, "You be careful for nothing." In other words, "Don't you fret or have any anxiety about anything."

If you should entertain worry or fret about your prayers, you will begin to nullify the effects of your praying. Give it to the Lord and let Him truly have it. Remember as long as you think you must have the problem, keeping you awake all night long trying to figure it out, He still does not have the problem. If the devil tries to bring up the issue again just say "No, I don't have that, devil. I don't have a care. I have given the whole problem to the Lord, and He has it."

Remember, He never slumbers or sleeps. Psalm 121:4 tells us that **"Behold, he that keepeth Israel shall neither slumber nor sleep."** You are His Beloved, because you are accepted in the Beloved, the Lord Jesus Christ. **"To the praise of the glory of his grace, wherein he hath made us accepted in the beloved"** (Ephesians 1:6). You can sleep in perfect assurance that He will work things out for you.

If we truly believe the Bible and practice God's Word, then we must understand that worry is useless. It needs to become a thing of the past. Jesus said, **"If ye shall ask any thing in my name, I will do it"** (John 14:14). As we let our faith soar, the things we have asked in faith will become a reality. God has everything under control as we commit all our worries and concerns to Him.

Things to consider:

All my worries, frets and concerns become a waste of my precious time when I consider the possibility of the Prayer of Commitment. God can handle things so much better than I can. He knows what is best, and as I give Him my troubles, all things will work out for the good.

Pray something like this:

Dear Heavenly Father, I come to You in the name of Jesus Christ. You know what I am going through at this particular time. I place all my concerns, burdens and worries into Your hands. Grant me the grace to leave these things with You. Lord, I do not want them back ever again in my life. In Christ's name. Amen.

Avoiding Thomas

<u>My verse for today is:</u>
"But ye, beloved, building up yourselves on your most holy faith, praying in the Holy Ghost" *(Jude 20)*.

"Then saith he to Thomas, Reach hither thy finger, and behold my hands; and reach hither thy hand, and thrust it into my side: and be not faithless but believing. And Thomas answered and said unto him, My Lord and my God. Jesus saith unto him, Thomas, because thou hast seen me, thou hast believed: blessed are they that have not seen, and yet have believed" (John 20:27-29).

We have expounded about prayer, but still there is one topic we must examine called "doubt." Thomas, a disciple, was an excellent example of one who had to confront his doubts. He was confronted head-on by Jesus Christ Himself. Thomas was told to touch His hands and His side. All doubt disappeared from Thomas when he did this.

At the same time, we must confront some of the problems we might be facing with prayer. One may ask, "Why wasn't I healed or why was there so much defeat, worry and frustration in my life? Why isn't my faith stronger?" The temptation to doubt God's Word is one of satan's main ways of stealing from the Christian what rightfully belongs to him. Doubt will rob the average Christian of his peace of mind, healing, material possessions, and the list gets longer.

There is a spiritual principle set forth in James 1:5 which is most appropriate in any situation of faith. *"If any of you lack wisdom, let him ask of God, that giveth to all men liberally, and upbraideth not; and it shall be given him. But let him ask in faith, nothing wavering* ('*doubting*' in Greek). *For he that wavereth (doubteth) is like a wave of the sea driven with the wind and tossed. For let not that man think that he shall receive any thing of the Lord."*

We may approach God in faith and believe what we have asked for will be granted, but if we should begin to doubt, satan will steal from us the answer. Remember, whatever God has promised to us from His Word can only be received by our faith in His ability to provide. Doubt can be like a cancer; it eats away at our faith. Faith is from God; doubt is from satan.

If you claim a promise of God, always be specific and ask in faith. Expect an answer, but remember it may not come the way you think. In the Prayer Inspired Life, we must come to the place where we do everything in faith believing God. *"What things soever ye desire, when ye pray, believe that ye receive them, and ye shall have them"* (Mark 11:24). *"If ye have faith, and doubt not...all things whatsoever ye shall ask in prayer, believing, ye shall receive"* (Matthew 21:21-22).

Learn to stop doubt the moment it comes into your mind. *Your defeat or victory will always be in your mind.* Satan will attempt to make you question whether you are worthy or have asked incorrectly. He may try to tell you that your illness is too far gone to receive a miracle from God. He may even tempt you to question whether God is really willing that you should be healed. This is the area in which you can experience great victory or great defeat. It is something that all of us have to experience and make choices. Refuse to doubt. **One minute of doubt could cost your prayer request.** Refuse to accept a single doubtful thought which he sends your way. ***"Resist the devil, and he will flee from you"*** (James 4:7).

When doubt knocks at the door of your mind, start praising God and begin to sing hymns of faith and victory. This is the most effective weapon we have at our disposal, and we all need to practice this. The practice of praising God will banish satan and his lies. Satan cannot tolerate a Christian who praises God all the time. He will flee from such a person.

One of the benefits of the Cross is the joy and praise purchased by the shed blood of Jesus Christ. When we praise God, there comes upon us a protective garment which the spirit of depression and doubt cannot penetrate. This is shown to us in Isaiah 61:1-3: ***"The Spirit of the Lord is upon me…to appoint unto them that mourn in Zion…the oil of joy for mourning, the garment of praise for the spirit of heaviness."***

Another important thing to remember is to never confess doubt or unbelief out loud. Always confess what God's Word has to say about any situation. Proverbs 18:21 says, ***"Death and life are in the power of the tongue."*** If you give into doubt even in a small way, it can stop faith and withhold God's blessings. Confessing doubt only opens the door for depression to enter into your mind and rob you of your peace and joy in the Lord.

Our tongues can become a great source of weakness, failure and defeat when we speak doubt. The confession of doubt is our personal admission that satan has defeated us. Always make an effort to be positive; it will change your life. As you live out the

Prayer Inspired Life, people will see that you have changed for the better since you have become a more positive person.

It is also very important that you associate with positive people. Stay away from those who are constantly confessing negative things. If you hang around doubters, know that satan could be speaking through them to cause your faith to weaken.

In the Prayer Inspired Life, the most effective way to overcome your doubts is to have a close walk with God. **"Faith cometh by hearing, and hearing by the word of God"** (Romans 10:17). Learn to pray so you will have the means of **"building up yourselves on your most holy faith"** (Jude 20).

Faith and doubt cannot exist together. Choose faith and your answers to prayer will be assured. Choose doubt and you will receive depression, unanswered prayer, illness, financial set-backs, etc.

Things to consider:

God so loves to hear me praise His holy name. *"Whoso offereth praise glorifieth me"* (Psalm 50:23). Doubts will leave the moment I start praising God. Praising God will cause satan to vanish since he can't stand my praises of God. Never for a moment will I let doubt dominate my thinking. I must always confess the positive about everything and every one. This will only show those around me that I have changed, and prayer and praise have helped me to do it.

Pray something like this:

Dear Heavenly Father, help me to be a positive person with praise on my lips for Your kindness and love. Help me overcome all my doubts, and let them be a thing of the past. May Your Word become unto me a treasure that I seek each day, as a Prayer Inspired Life becomes a reality to me. I ask all of this in Christ's name. Amen.

Hearing the Voice of the Holy Spirit

<u>My verse for today is</u>:
"But the Comforter, which is the Holy Ghost, whom the Father will send in my name, he shall teach you all things, and bring all things to your remembrance, whatsoever I have said unto you" (John 14:26).

As we learn the art of prayer, we become aware that there are times God wants to speak to us. God will speak to us occasionally by direct means, but most often, He communicates His will to us indirectly. Oftentimes it is in the form of an inward knowing or witness in our spirit, or it may come as an inner voice from the Holy Spirit. At other times the Holy Spirit will give us the guidance that we need by the illumination in our minds to understand and interpret some portion of Scripture, which He will direct us to, or by giving us the necessary wisdom that we might desperately need. He will give us insight to make the correct decision concerning some matter which we have been praying about for some time.

We need to grasp the truth that it is in the realm of indirect revelation that the importance of being completely yielded to the Holy Spirit is so evident. To the extent one is yielded to the Spirit will he be sensitive to His voice when He speaks; and to the extent one is sensitive to His voice, will the believer be able to respond.

Today, there are many voices seeking to influence the believer, some of which are from God and some are definitely not from the Lord. Unless one is fully yielded to the Holy Spirit, he may be so insensitive to the voice of the Holy Spirit that he can be easily deceived and ensnared into something which is false.

When Rita and I lived in England, we raised German shepherd dogs which we enjoyed very much. The small puppies would respond to anyone who would call them and give them something to eat. Our more mature dogs would not respond at all since they did not know the people. They would only respond to those who took care of them. The mature dogs did not get this way by running and playing with other dogs, but it was the result of devoting long hours in discipline and training, learning to obey and respond to the voice of their masters.

Everyone who prays will become sensitive to the Holy Spirit to one degree or another. Patience is required to learn how to hear the voice of the Spirit. At this present time God is preparing an end time army of saints for the spiritual warfare that lies just ahead of us. This army will consist of men and women who will be so sensitive to the voice of the Spirit that they will respond immediately and obey without any questions. They will be like a modern day computer; they will have the ability to filter out that which is false, and sense any error immediately. It will not be necessary for them to call the pastor and ask if this or that doctrine is scriptural, or whether some prophecy which they have heard is true or false, or whether some task they feel led to undertake is of God, the flesh or the devil.

However, the only way the believer will be able to become this sensitive will be through total consecration to our Lord and fully yielded to His Spirit. We find that many Christians are not trained in the Scriptures and are so insensitive to the voice of the Spirit that many frequently reject what God is saying to them. They allow themselves to be deceived by what is false and unscriptural, just as Jesus predicted would occur in the end times (Matthew 24:11-14; 2 Timothy 4:1-4).

Satan will do all that he can to deceive both believers and non-believers. This is frequently his strategy to attempt to deceive the gullible. Others are being led astray by the error taught by some today that there is to be no bodily resurrection or literal visible return and appearance of Christ. Some teach that those saints in heaven are now growing in the Spirit and being changed to eventually rule and reign on planet earth. Christ supposedly is to rule and reign through them. We find others, in a time when we are witnessing the revival of all forms of the occult, being deluded by the teachings that the charismatic gift of the Word of knowledge and ESP are the same psychic gift under different terminology. Many are so untrained in the things of the Spirit, they believe everything supernatural is from God, and everyone who prophesies, has a vision or predicts the future, is a bona-fide prophet of God.

In order to mature in faith and become effective instruments in God's hands, it is necessary for us to learn how to recognize the inner witness of our spirits, as well as discern the voice of the Holy Spirit. There are two basic ways by which God leads and directs His people, whether in answer to some prayer for guidance, or in order to fulfill His will and purpose in our lives. We find that God endeavors to speak to His people by means of the voice of the Holy Spirit in order to direct, guide, teach or influence them along some particular line, but since they have not been taught how to discern His voice, He often goes unheeded. Jesus said, **"My sheep hear my voice, and I know them, and they follow me"** (John 10:27). How can they follow Him if they do not know how to discern His voice? He certainly did not mean to shout from heaven what He wants for them. He wants to direct and guide each of us, but He did promise that He would speak to them by His Spirit, which would be within them. **"Howbeit, when he, the Spirit of truth is come, he will**

guide you into all truth" (John 16:13), and "**He shall teach you all things**" (John 14:26).

Some Christians are waiting for God to give them a revelation through a vision or prophecy concerning His will for them, or regarding some important matter about which they are praying when, if they only realized it, God is really trying to communicate His will to them by His Spirit within them. If they would spend a little more time in His Word and in prayer, and be willing to discern His voice and hear Him speak inwardly to their spirit, they would have the needed direction or an answer to some prayer.

The purpose of the Holy Spirit speaking to your spirit is to guide, admonish, teach, warn or influence you concerning some matter about which you may or may not be praying about. On occasion, the Spirit has spoken inwardly to me to speak to a particular individual concerning a spiritual matter, or has directed me to write someone about his or her personal problems or situation.

There is an interesting phrase, "The Holy Spirit said...." There are at least four passages in the New Testament where the voice and guidance of the Holy Spirit are explicitly stated to have been given. These passages are found in the Book of Acts 8:29;10:19; 13:2 and 16:6-7. We may confidently assume that these instances stand out from a background of common experiences.

First of all, the Holy Spirit spoke to men of willing obedience (Philip) and of devotion to the Gospel (Paul). In the entire assembly at Antioch, He spoke during a time of waiting upon God in priestly service and fasting. All of this teaches us that hearing the voice of the Spirit demands spiritual qualifications in both individuals and congregations.

The means by which He spoke is most interesting. In the case of Philip and Peter, those who heard the Spirit's voice were entirely alone at the time. In the case of Antioch, there is a possibility that He spoke through one of the "certain prophets" (Acts 13:1), though this is not stated. There is some possibility that He may have spoken through Silas, a "prophet" (Acts 15:32), when "forbidding" Paul to preach in Asia. The subsequent vision of the man of Macedonia came to Paul personally (Acts 16:10), and it is scripturally safe to believe that the previous hindrance from the Holy Spirit had also been conveyed to the leader of the missionary band directly and personally.

There is one profound truth in each of the cases that have been cited in Scripture, and that is, each time He spoke it had something to do with the furtherance of the Gospel. He spoke to the early saints to prepare them to preach the Gospel to the world of their day. He spoke in total unity of the Godhead. All that was spoken was totally in accord with the Word of God. The Holy Spirit will always speak in accord with the purposes of the Godhead. This is one way of knowing if you are hearing the Holy Spirit or some other spirit.

Here we need to stress the inward witness and the inner voice of the Spirit are not merely some feelings or insight you might have about some matter. Feelings have nothing to do with the leading of the Spirit. When we are in deep prayer, we become aware of the inner witness of the Spirit. Oftentimes the Holy Spirit is trying to get our attention about matters we need to discern. In every instance, what we experience will bypass the mind or the intellect. Please understand that the witness within our spirit and the inner voice of the Holy Spirit, may at times, go contrary to our personal "feelings" or "emotions" regarding some issue, but we will know what God's will is concerning the situation and what we should do.

The Holy Spirit will speak to each of us when He so desires. Our duty is to be spiritually prepared to hear and receive what He might be saying. The Prayer Inspired Life is a life full of the Holy Spirit and His divine directions. It is the only life that makes any sense today in this world so full of confusion.

Things to consider:

The Holy Spirit wants to speak to me. He wishes to guide me into all that God has for me. I want only what God wants for me. My life can only have meaning in Christ. As I humbly seek Him in prayer, He will show me the secret treasures of goodness and the love God has for all of His Creation.

Pray something like this:

Dear Precious Heavenly Father, I have received the Holy Spirit by being born again. Now Lord, let that Precious Guest, the Holy Spirit who lives in me, have His perfect way in all things in my life. I ask this in the name of Jesus Christ, my Savior.

Open Heaven

<u>My verse for today is</u>:
"For ever, O Lord, thy word is settled in heaven" *(Psalm 119:89)*.

Our school of prayer has come to an end, but a life of prayer awaits all those who would allow God to become more intimate with them. What we have learned about prayer must now be put into practice in our lives.

The Prayer Inspired Life is a life lived in a new spiritual dimension. It is a life that is filled with the supernatural God who beckons to each of us to come up higher. Let us fly up to God using our wings of faith and surrender to His supernatural realm of peace, joy and tranquility. He beckons us to join Him above our circumstances, and He will show us the end result of our prayers if we will only go to Him and "be still and know that I (He is) am God."

The Prayer Inspired Life is a life full of meaning and purpose, which the entire world is seeking. We have the ability, through prayer, to have an audience with the King of Glory. He bids us come into the Holy of Holies where His love abounds beyond measure. Love is the essence of His being and life. He asks us to share in this with Him. He excuses our earthly mannerisms and receives us any time we come into His presence.

When we come to God in prayer, He shows us the splendor of His Being. Each time He gives some new light to enlighten our minds, and some new delight to fill our hearts. The greatest souls of all time have cherished their time with the King in prayer. Now it is our golden opportunity to experience what the old saints found most difficult to put into language. They put in writing their great joy of the ecstasy they encountered with the Lord.

Again, our Lord awaits all of us to enter into deep prayer so we might once again see His goodness on our behalf. The Prayer Inspired Life is like none other, because it causes one to become caught up with Divinity. Prayer unites us with God, blots out our sin, and preserves us from temptation.

While practicing the Prayer Inspired Life, one begins to see the hand of God moving in mysterious ways, and realizes the heavens are full of miracles wanting to be released if only someone will take the time to pray. The world wants to see God in action! The praying saint can display this divine intervention through prayer. Prayer is the only vehicle that will open the heavens to loose the mercy of God on this sin sick world.

As we choose the Prayer Inspired Life, we are advertising God's great love and mercy toward His Creation. No one is beyond the reach of the Holy Spirit. The heavens are waiting upon us to call forth the immeasurable treasures of grace for the salvation of multitudes.

The Prayer Inspired Life is a life given to God that shows the presence of the indwelling Christ without ever having to say a word. Those who accept this new lifestyle will radiate the glory of God! Nothing is impossible with God. The treasures of heaven will be opened to those who will take the time to pray. God wants a praying people to believe Him for the impossible.

Indeed, the sound of the trumpet is about to be blown from heaven. It is time for the harvest of souls. The challenge of this hour is greater than ever before. Who will pray for the harvest? Who will live the Prayer Inspired Life? The Prayer Inspired Life will once again show the world the beauty of holiness. It will show the life of Christ in action through us.

Things to consider:

I am the only one who can choose the Prayer Inspired Life. It will mean leaving a life of mediocrity in favor of excellence in the Spirit. Everything in my life will change for the better as I choose this new lifestyle.

Pray something like this:

Dear Heavenly Father, my heart has been stirred by reading this book. Lord Jesus, I want You totally; nothing and no one else will suffice. I choose the Prayer Inspired Life that I might better come to know You and love You. May the heavens open as You pour down Your grace upon me to enrich the quality of my life. In Christ's name I pray. Amen.

Bibliography

Bounds, E. M. *Power Through Prayer* (1962). Reprint. Grand Rapids. Zondervan, 1976.

Conner, Kevin J. *The Foundations of Christian Doctrine.* Kent, England. Sovereign World International; Portland. BT Publishing, 1980.

Dearing, Frank P. *About God and People.* Jacksonville. Higley Publishing Corp. 1972.

Guillarent, Dom Augustin. *The Prayers of the Presence of God.* Wilkes- Barre. Dimension Books, 1965.

Kenyon, E. W. *In His Presence.* Seattle. Kenyon's Gospel Publishing Society, 1969.

MacGregor, Jerry & Prys, Marie. *1001 Surprising Things You Should Know About God.* Grand Rapids. Baker Books, 2003.

Moffatt, James. *The Moffatt Translation Of The Bible.* (1949) London. Hodder & Stoughton Ltd. 1972.

Rea, John. *The Holy Spirit in the Bible* (1990). Lake Mary, FL. Creation House, 1992.

Richardson, Alan. *A Theological Word Book of the Bible.* (1950). New York. The Macmillan Company, 1967.

Sanders, J. Oswald. *Prayer Power Unlimited.* (1977) East Sussex, England. Highland Books, 1985.

Strong, James. *Strong's Exhaustive Concordance*. Royal Publishing. Nashville, 1979.

Thayer, H. J. *Thayer's Greek-English Lexicon of the New Testament*. Grand Rapids. Baker Book House, 1977.

Footnotes

God
1 [1] Jerry Macgregor & Marie Prys, <u>1001 Surprising Things You Should Know About God</u>, (Baker Books, Grand Rapids, MI., 2004), 105.

God the Creator
1[2] Ibid., 105.
2[3] Ibid., 105.

Creation
1[4] John Rea, <u>The Holy Spirit in the Bible,</u> (Creation House, Lake Mary, Florida, 1990), 29.
2[5] Ibid., 31.
3[6] Ibid., 31.
4[7] James H. Strong, <u>Strong's Exhaustive Concordance</u>, (Royal Publishers, Inc., Nashville, Tennessee), 47.

God is Able
1[8] Joseph H. Thayer, <u>Thayer's Greek-English Lexicon of the New Testament</u>, 117.

The Infallible Word
1[9] E. M. Bounds, <u>Power Through Prayer</u>, (Zondervan Publishing House, Grand Rapids, Michigan, 1976), 85.

Heart, Mind and Soul
1[10] Kevin J. Conner, <u>The Foundations of Christian Doctrine</u>, (Sovereign World International, Kent, England, 1980), 125.
2[11] Ibid., 125.
3[12] Ibid., 125.

How To Love God

1[13] Frank P. Dearing, <u>About God And People</u>, (Higley Publishing Corp, Jacksonville, FL, 1972), 31.

2[14] Ibid., 66.

What is Prayer?

1[15] E. W. Kenyon, <u>In His Presence</u>, (Kenyon's Gospel Publishing Society Inc., Seattle, Washington, 1969), 7.

2[16] Dom Augustin Guillerand, <u>The Prayer Of The Presence Of God</u>, (Dimension Books, Wilkes-Barre, Pennsylvania, 1966), 46.

3[17] J. Oswald Sanders, <u>Prayer Power Unlimited</u>, (Highland Books, East Sussex, England, 1977), 9.

4[18] Ibid., 13.

5[19] Ibid., 21.

6[20] Ibid., 27.

7[21] Ibid., 29.

Claiming Your Promises

1[22] J. Oswald Sanders, <u>Prayer Power Unlimited</u>, (Highland Books, Moody Press, East Sussex, England, 1977), 39.

2[23] E. W. Kenyon, <u>In His Presence</u>, (Kenyon's Gospel Publishing Society, Seattle, WA, 1969), 51.

Dr. Michael L. McCann
P.O. Box 1386
Bay City, MI 48706

24 hour Internet TV channel:
www.prayerinspired.tv

Join Dr. McCann and other guests for prayer and teaching on prayer. Your life will never be the same as you learn to pray with authority, knowledge and power. Watch www.prayerinspired.tv anytime of day or night online 24 hours a day.

Website:
www.doctormccann.com

www.ingramcontent.com/pod-product-compliance
Lightning Source LLC
Chambersburg PA
CBHW032123090426
42743CB00007B/438